Brian Johnson B

The Musical Journey and Life of a Legend

This book is for:

....

....

....

....

....

Copyright © 2023
All rights reserved

The content of this book may not be reproduced, duplicated, or transmitted without the author's or publisher's express written permission. Under no circumstances will the publisher or author be held liable or legally responsible for any damages, reparation, or monetary loss caused by the information contained in this book, whether directly or indirectly.

Legal Notice:

This publication is copyrighted. It is strictly for personal use only. You may not change, distribute, sell, use, quote, or paraphrase any part of this book without the author's or publisher's permission.

Disclaimer Notice:

Please keep in mind that the information in this document is only for educational and entertainment purposes. Every effort has been made to present accurate, up-to-date, reliable, and comprehensive information. There are no express or implied warranties. Readers understand that the author is not providing legal, financial, medical, or professional advice. This book's content was compiled from a variety of sources. Please seek the advice of a licensed professional before attempting any of the techniques described in this book. By reading this document, the reader agrees that the author is not liable for any direct or indirect losses incurred as a result of using the information contained within this document, including, but not limited to, errors, omissions, or inaccuracies.

TABLE OF CONTENTS

Part One
1. Out in the Cold
2. A-Wop Bop A-Loo Bop
3. A Ruff Business
4. Crashes and Fires

Part Two
5. Oops
6. A Horrible Shit Shower
7. Highway to . . . Nowhere
8. Stowaway
9. A Message from Above

Part Three
10. Beautiful Mover
11. Breaking Up
12. Greetings from Paradise
13. Back from Black
14. The Last Bit before the End

Part One:
1. Out in the Cold

It all started with a silent documentary called Nanook of the North, which I watched on our brand-new black-and-white television. The video was created in the 1920s and can still be found on the internet today. It must have been played on the BBC because it was the only thing our rooftop antenna could pick up at the time. (The North East didn't get television until six years after the war.)

Normally, I was uninterested in television. It was mostly horticultural shows and church organ recitals, and if you were lucky, re-runs of Gregory Peck movies and Mickey Mouse cartoons - dull, dreadful crap that you couldn't pay me to watch instead of playing outside with my pals. But Nanook of the North was different. It was riveting. The star of it was this Inuk guy named Nanook who lived in the Canadian Arctic, and you got to see him building an igloo, hunting for seals and eating the blubber, and fighting a polar bear - all while a blizzard was raging, ice was cracking under his feet, and it was twenty below freezing. And he carried a large hunting knife and had this lovely Inuk wife and a cute little Inuk baby who wore a small fur hat. And because it was winter in Dunston and snowing, my mind ran wild.

When the movie ended, I raced outside into the snow and declared to myself, 'Right, I'm going to build an igloo like Nanook's.' So I did. It was fantastic. About five feet wide and five feet tall, with a small opening in the front for crawling in and out.

But the trouble with doing something so exciting in the late afternoon when you're a kid is that you end up lying in bed, wide awake, mind racing, long after everyone else has gone to bed. That's exactly what occurred - and why I decided in the middle of the night that there was no danger in walking outside in the dark to take one last quick look at what I'd built. So I threw on a jumper over my pyjamas, grabbed my dad's torch, and crept out the back door and into the garden. And as I slid into my igloo, I stopped being Brian Johnson in the back garden of his council house in Dunston and became Brianook of the North East, unwinding after a long day of seal hunting and a feast of blubber pie. Then I yawned like Nanook, which was a major mistake since it made me realize how fatigued I was, and I passed out like a light.

Being sent home by your teacher was a guarantee of a big, belt-whipping bollocking, but I was feeling so bad that it wasn't even on my mind. As I walked back to Beech Drive after school, I got slower and slower... until my feet couldn't take it anymore. I had no idea what was going on with me. I mean, I used to run everywhere at full speed, but now I couldn't even stand on my own two feet. I ended up just sitting on the ground and curling up into a ball. Brianook of the North East was preparing to face his end.

That's when I heard the voice of a compassionate elderly lady who'd discovered me laying on the street.
'Could you give us your name, dear?'

We didn't even have a phone at the time, let alone a car, so when the Good Samaritan of Dunston dropped me down at home, my mother had to leave me alone in front of the fire and dash to the nearest phone box to call our local GP, dear old Dr. Fairbairn. He told her he'd be right over; he just needed to eat some lunch first, then finish with his surgery patients, which would take, oh, about five hours.

He finally arrived about 5 p.m. By this point, I was moaning, sweating, and freezing cold, and I was having problems breathing. Dr. Fairbairn declared that I was 'gravely unwell' and rolled me over to give me an injection in my buttocks to stabilize me. He stayed with me until well after midnight, which was unheard of. 'I need you to be a brave soldier tonight, okay Brian?' Before giving me another shot, I recall him stating. Then he inquired if I loved vehicles.

I didn't simply like vehicles. My father used to call me "car daft." They were extremely uncommon back then. There was just one car on our block, a Morris Minor owned by my father's boss. I could stare at it for hours, envisioning myself traveling through my own Neverland. In fact, my father became so tired of me talking about automobiles and trying to find new cars to gawk at on the street that

he went to our local garage and asked if they would give him a steering wheel. (The only requirement is that it not have originated from a German vehicle.) He ended up obtaining one for sixpence, which he took out of my pocket money, and then he bought a huge stick, pushed it through our bedhead, linked it to the steering wheel, and heaped pillows up around it like a driving seat. I must have put at least 50,000 miles on the bed.
'Yes, I enjoy vehicles,' I moaned to Dr. Fairbairn.

'Well, I'm delighted to hear that, son,' he smiled. 'Because, between you and me, I just bought a new Rover. And if you can stay strong and improve, I'll give you a ride in it.'

Behind him, I could see my parents looking at me and holding hands, which terrified me because they never held hands. I'd never seen my father's expression before. I suppose it was love. And fear. Both of which were things that a man like my father would never let anyone see. There was also a peculiar sense of resignation. I mean, it wasn't uncommon for my father's generation to lose a child to the flu, tuberculosis, or even strep throat. He appeared to be thinking, "Well, there's the first one to go."

Of course, my father should have realized that a Rover was about equivalent to a Rolls-Royce in those days. It had chrome dials and a mahogany dashboard, as well as an AM radio built in. Furthermore, its engine was so strong that it could accelerate from zero to sixty mph in under twenty seconds... on its way to a high speed of almost eighty mph!
So there was no way I was going to let myself die and miss out on that.

Apart from my near-death incident with the igloo, life on Beech Drive was a vast improvement over Oak Avenue. Just a few days after we came - this was at No. 106 - I remember waking up to see these flags everywhere, tables and chairs on the streets, and everyone throwing a tremendous party because we had a new Queen. Of course, it rained for the majority of the day, but no one seemed to mind. They even butchered and barbecued a pig in Dunston Park. And, on top of that, everyone received a free mug. It's difficult to put into words how mind-blowing that was in a period when bacon was rationed. If everyone on our street can get a free cup, then literally anything is possible in this place!

The street still had gas lights, which were ignited every night by a man with a huge stick. And there was still a rag-and-bone man - 'the rag man,' we called him - who had a little cart pulled by a sad-looking horse with a balloon tied to its reins. I'll never forget the day I understood that if you gave the rag man an old jumper or a bedsheet, you got a penny or a balloon. Why hadn't anyone told me about this before? But, of course, as soon as my mother saw what I was up to, she was chasing the rag man halfway up the street, attempting to reclaim a pair of my father's old socks.

We had so much fun back then. We were free in ways that you couldn't conceive now, back when there were no automobiles, no traffic, no glowing displays and video games to become hopelessly addicted to, and when everyone looked out for everyone else's kids. Because everyone had tiny housing, youngsters lived outside, made their own entertainment, and established their own little gangs.

Even school - Dunston Hill infants, followed by juniors - wasn't all that horrible.
Every day, the Bigs would walk the Littles there and back in shorts, rain, drizzle, sleet, hail, snow, anything. I'd add 'shine,' but I can count the number of times I saw the sun in Dunston throughout my boyhood on one hand.

One of the reasons I liked babies' school so much was the classroom, which contained a seesaw and a small roundabout, both of which made the kids vomit. Mr. Graham, the caretaker, was always standing nearby with a mop and bucket.

When playtime was complete, Mrs. Patterson would give us each a small blackboard and a bit of chalk to practice writing our ABCs. Then we'd have music classes, with all the females getting recorders and all the boys getting triangles and tambourines.

Because I enjoyed tingling my triangle, that was the beginning of a lifelong love of music for me. I could do it for hours. And we'd sing songs while Mrs. Patterson played the piano. 'Underneath the Spreading Chestnut Tree' is awful. But it didn't matter to me. Mrs. Patterson might have whatever song she wanted as long as I could tickle my triangle.

English was my strongest subject. I enjoyed writing and always received high scores for my stories and essays - and when I got a gold star, I'd bring it home to show my mother and father.
But it was after school that life truly began.

Every night, no matter how hard it rained, we'd set up our jumpers in the center of the street as goalposts and play football. When it snowed, the street became a battleground, and we'd have snowball fights that lasted for hours.

My father took me to my first football game. It wasn't a Newcastle United game, though, because tickets would have cost an arm and a leg, and St. James's Park was at least a thirty-minute bus journey away. Instead, we went to adjacent Redheugh Park to witness United's poor cousins, Gateshead AFC, which charged only tuppence at the gate and drew a couple of thousand people on a good day.

My father bought a 'cracket,' a small wooden stool with wickerwork on top, which he placed near the wall at the edge of the pitch so I could stand on it and look over.
What I remember most is marveling at all the worn and peeling old 1930s advertisements that were still on the wall. Things like, 'You know it's wise to use Bovril to keep pneumonia and chills at bay!' Some of them had been painted on metal backing, and the paint had gradually chipped away, revealing rust. But they were the only splashes of color in an otherwise gloomy world, and that captivated me.

We had one of those old gramophones with the steel needle that you wound up with a crank handle, and every now and then my father would put on one of these archaic 78s - although, to be honest, he never really cared for music. The only one I recall is 'A Bird in a

Gilded Cage' by Harry Anthony, who had this awful, warbly, strangled-sounding tenor voice. Over the hiss, you couldn't hear much. I couldn't take it anymore. In fact, my brothers and I ended up taking the records and throwing them one by one over the fence in our back garden, which was a lot more fun than it sounds because if you flicked your wrist when you threw them, the 78s would spin around and float for a bit in the air before coming down gently. We basically turned Harry Anthony into a Frisbee, which was really astounding because the Frisbee hadn't even been developed yet.

My musical tastes were molded totally by the BBC Radio show Children's Favourites, hosted by the somewhat stiff and Victorian-sounding 'Uncle Mac'. Every program would begin with him saying, 'Hello children, everywhere,' followed by one of the finest BBC theme melodies of all time, 'Puffin' Billy' by the Melodi Light Orchestra.
Every Saturday morning, beginning at 9.10 a.m., Uncle Mac would play songs like 'The Laughing Policeman' or 'I Taut I Taw a Puddy Tat' by Mel Blanc, the man who voiced the majority of the Looney Tunes characters, with a little Bing Crosby and Max Bygraves thrown in for good measure. If you were lucky and Uncle Mac was feeling bold, you might even get to hear one of Frank Sinatra's or Doris Day's tamer songs.

It was the highlight of my week.
Christmases are some of my most vivid and enchanting recollections of growing up in Dunston, even though we couldn't afford a turkey, much alone genuine presents back then.

Every year, without fail, my father would leave a biscuit and a glass of milk for Santa Claus, and once we were all in bed, he'd take a bite out of the biscuit and guzzle down the milk, leaving sooty fingerprints everywhere from the coal in the fireplace. Sergeant Johnson was a huge softy at heart, despite his rough exterior. And, of course, my brothers and I would lie awake for what seemed like an eternity, shouting out, 'Dad?!' 'Has he been yet?' at fifteen-minute intervals beginning at 3 a.m. 'Go to bed!' would come the muffled response... until my father eventually cracked and escorted us downstairs at the crack of morning.

When it came to presents, you could never go wrong with an orange wrapped in tinfoil at the bottom of your stocking (to make it look 'Christmassy') and a bar of Fry's Five Boys milk chocolate or, if you were really lucky, a Cadbury's Chocolate Selection Box, which looked incredibly exciting when wrapped in wrapping paper simply because it was so large.

The gifts got better over time (including a lovely, very grown-up Raleigh bicycle), until one Christmas, Santa Claus sent a 'family present' that changed my life - an Elizabethan reel-to-reel tape recorder with a little plug-in microphone.

That tape recorder changed everything. I could suddenly place the microphone near the radio's speaker and record Children's Favorites, allowing me to listen to the songs whenever I wished. But, as usual, there was a problem... which arrived in the guise of our pet budgerigar, whose name was either Bobby or Peter, I can't remember which. Everyone had a budgie back then, and they were all named Bobby or Peter. People enjoyed them because they could be taught to say things like 'Whey aye, man' and 'Alreet pet,' and since they just ate seeds, making them one of the cheapest sources of entertainment available.
Anyway, this bird got into the habit of singing every time the radio came on. He enjoyed Children's Favourites almost as much as I did. And he was very, very loud.

It didn't help that the tiny microphone could only pick up high tones and had no bass at all. So, when I played back my first recording of Uncle Mac's program, all I could hear was a distant and muffled James Baskett singing 'Zip-a-Dee-Doo-Dah' with this dreadful high-pitched whistling over the top.

Moving the budgie to another room didn't help because it merely made him upset, and when he was upset, the tiny gentleman began squawking at twice the regular volume.
After a while, I gave up and just started singing into the microphone myself, which didn't bother the budgie in the same way. At first, the only songs that sprang to mind were the same corny ones we sang in

school. But I couldn't stop recording myself since it was so much fun. I discovered that I could slow or speed up the tape, making me sound like a deep-voiced old guy or Alvin the Chipmunk. I spent most of that Christmas in the bedroom I shared with my brothers, singing into the microphone while watching the tape reels run around, then rewinding, playing it back, and starting over - or adding something else - until my father must have begun to regret ever getting the blasted thing. 'Like the sound of your own voice, do you?' he huffed at one point.

I flushed bright crimson and murmured something. But the correct answer - which I was far too humiliated to acknowledge - was yes, I do. It was the novelty of it that drew me in, the feeling of making something new and being the first to hear it.

I just never grew tired of it.
I'm still not tired of it today.

2. A-Wop Bop A-Loo Bop

It all started with a silent film called Nanook of the North, which I saw on our brand-new black-and-white television. The video was shot in the 1920s and may still be found on the internet today. It must have been broadcast on the BBC because it was the only thing our rooftop aerial could pick up at the time. (Television did not reach the North East until six years after the war.)

Normally, I was uninterested in watching television. It was mostly horticultural shows and church organ recitals, and if you were lucky, reruns of Gregory Peck movies and Mickey Mouse cartoons - dull, dreadful crap that you couldn't pay me to watch instead of playing outside with my pals. But Nanook of the North was unique. It was engrossing. The star of it was this Inuk guy named Nanook who lived in the Canadian Arctic, and you got to see him build an igloo, hunt for seals and eat the blubber, and fight a polar bear - all while a blizzard was raging, ice was cracking under his feet, and it was twenty degrees below zero. And he carried a large hunting knife and had a beautiful Inuk wife and a pretty little Inuk infant wearing a fur hat. And because it was winter in Dunston and it was snowing, my mind ran wild.

When the movie ended, I raced outside into the snow and told myself, 'Right, I'm going to build an igloo like Nanook's.' So I did it. And it was fantastic. About five feet wide and the same height, with a little opening in the front for crawling in and out.

But the trouble with doing something so exciting in the late afternoon when you're a kid is that you end up laying there in bed, mind racing, long after everyone else has gone to bed. That's exactly what occurred - and why, in the middle of the night, I figured it wouldn't hurt to step outside in the dark to take one last quick look at what I'd built. So I threw on a jumper over my pyjamas, grabbed my father's torch, and crept out the back door and into the garden. And as I got into my igloo, I transitioned from Brian Johnson in the back garden of his council house in Dunston to Brianook of the North East, unwinding after a long day of seal hunting and a feast of blubber pie. Then I yawned like Nanook, which was a major mistake since it made me realize how tired I was, and I passed out like a light.

Being sent home by your teacher was a surefire way to get a major, belt-whipping bollocking, but I was in such a bad mood that it wasn't even on my mind. As I walked back to Beech Drive after school, I got slower and slower... until my feet couldn't take it any longer. I had no idea what was going on. I mean, I used to run everywhere at top speed, but now I couldn't even stand on my own two feet. I ended myself sitting on the ground and curling up into a ball. Brianook of the North East was almost ready to meet his end.

That's when I heard the voice of a compassionate elderly lady who had discovered me laying on the street.
'Could you just tell us your name, dear?'

We didn't even have a phone or a car at the time, so when the Good Samaritan of Dunston dropped me down at home, my mother had to leave me alone in front of the fire and dash to the nearest phone box to call our local GP, dear old Dr. Fairbairn. He said he'd be right over; he just needed to eat some lunch first, then finish with his surgery patients, which would take approximately five hours.

When he arrived, it was around 5 p.m. I was moaning, sweating, and freezing cold by this point, and I was having difficulties breathing. Dr. Fairbairn declared that I was 'gravely unwell' and flipped me over to give me a buttock injection to stabilize me. He stayed with me until well after midnight, which was unprecedented. 'I need you to be a strong soldier tonight, Brian,' says the commander. Before giving me another injection, he said something to me. He then inquired if I loved vehicles.

Well, I wasn't only about vehicles. My father used to call me a 'car daft'. They were extremely rare back then. There was just one on our street, a Morris Minor owned by my father's boss. I could gaze at it for hours, envisioning myself traveling through my own Neverland. In fact, my father became so tired of me talking about automobiles and looking for new cars to gawk at on the street that he went to our

neighborhood garage and asked if they would give him a steering wheel. (The only condition is that it did not come from a German vehicle.) He eventually purchased one for sixpence, which he deducted from my pocket money, and then he grabbed a huge stick, pushed it through our bedhead, hooked it to the steering wheel, and heaped pillows up around it like a driving seat. That bed must have gotten at least 50,000 miles from me.
I moaned to Dr. Fairbairn, "Yes, I like cars."

'Well, I'm pleased to hear that, son,' he said cheerfully. 'Because, between you and me, I recently purchased a new Rover. And if you can stay strong and improve, I'll take you for a spin in it.'

I could see my parents looking at me and holding hands behind him, which terrified me because they never held hands. My father's expression, in particular, was something I'd never seen before. It was, well, I suppose... love. And terror. Both of which were things that a man like my father would never show anyone. There was also an odd sense of resignation. For my father's generation, losing a child to the flu, TB, or even strep throat was not uncommon. He seemed to be thinking, "Well, there's the first one to go."

Of course, my father should have realized that a Rover in those days was about equivalent to a Rolls-Royce. It had chrome dials and a mahogany dashboard, as well as an AM radio. Furthermore, its engine was so strong that it could go from zero to sixty mph in less than twenty seconds... on its way to a high speed of almost eighty mph!
So there was no way in hell I was going to let myself die and miss out on it.

Aside from my near-death incident with the igloo, living on Beech Drive was vastly superior to Oak Avenue. Just a few days after we moved there - this was at No. 106 - I remember waking up to see these flags everywhere, tables and chairs on the streets, and everyone throwing a tremendous party because we had a new Queen. Of course, it rained for the majority of the day, but no one cared. They even killed and barbecued a pig in Dunston Park. On top of that, everyone received a free mug. It's difficult to put into words how mind-blowing that was during a period when bacon was rationed. I thought to myself, "Bloody hell, if everyone on our street can get a free mug, then anything is possible in this place!"

The street still had gas lights, which were ignited every night by a man wielding a large stick. And there was still a rag-and-bone man, dubbed "the rag man," who had a tiny cart pulled by a sad-looking horse with a balloon tied to its reins. I'll never forget the day I understood that if you gave the rag man an old sweater or a bedsheet, you got a cent or a balloon in exchange. Why hadn't anyone ever told me about this before? But, of course, as soon as my mother saw what I was up to, she was chasing the rag man halfway up the street, attempting to reclaim a pair of my father's old socks.

The amount of fun we had back then was incredible. We were free in a way that you couldn't conceive now, back when there were no automobiles, no traffic, no glowing displays and video games to become hopelessly addicted to, and when everyone looked out for everyone else's kids. Because everyone had tiny houses, the youngsters lived outside, created their own amusement, and established their own little gangs.

Even school - Dunston Hill infants, followed by juniors - wasn't all that horrible in the grand scheme of things.
Every day, the Big ones would walk the Little ones there and back in shorts, rain, drizzle, sleet, hail, snow, anything. I'd add 'shine,' but I can count the number of times I saw the sun in Dunston as a child on one hand.

One of the reasons I liked babies' school so much was the classroom, which included a seesaw and a small circular that made the kids vomit. Mr. Graham, the caretaker, was always standing nearby, mop and bucket in hand.

Mrs. Patterson would give us each a small blackboard and a bit of chalk when playtime was done so we could practice writing our ABCs. Then we'd have music lessons, with the girls getting recorders and the lads getting triangles and tambourines.

Because I enjoyed tingling my triangle, that was the start of a lifelong passion of music for me. It's something I could do for hours. And Mrs. Patterson would play the piano as we sang songs. 'Underneath the Spreading Chestnut Tree' is terrible. But I didn't mind. I'd sing whatever Mrs. Patterson wanted as long as I could tingle my triangle.

My favorite subject was English. I like writing and always received high scores for my stories and essays - and when I received a gold star, I'd bring it home to show my mother and father.

But it wasn't until after school that life truly began.

After a few years on Beech Drive, my mother's homesickness began to fade. Perhaps it was just that she'd found a market for it - an Italian food-importing company in Glasgow managed by a guy named Pietro Fazzi, who'd been imprisoned with his brothers by the British throughout the war, then released after VE Day.

Every Friday afternoon, my mother would ring in her order from a phone box across the street, and I'd spend hours listening to her talking to Mr. Fazzi in Italian. A few days later, a man would appear on our doorway to give her goods, and my mother would beam like a child on Christmas morning.

I'll never forget the first time she prepared her Italian doughnuts, known as bomboloni because they resemble miniature bombs, on a Sunday afternoon. The entire family sat and watched the dough rise in front of the fire, a damp towel carefully placed over it, as if it were a scene from a Hollywood film. Then she kneaded it, cut it into small rounds, delicately put out the doughnuts on parchment paper, and gently fried them in the best oil Mr. Fazzi could find. And then they came out, all warm and soft and incredibly delicious-looking, and she cut out the centers as a special treat for the kids, rolled them in sugar, and you couldn't believe how fantastic they tasted! My brothers and I could have devoured a zillion of them.

And, of course, the bomboloni was smelt by the neighbors from halfway up the street, and they'd never smelled anything like it before, so they all ran over. And by then, my mother had finished her third or fourth batch, so she began wrapping the doughnuts in old

newspaper and handing them out, and before I knew it, I was taking them into school for Mrs. Patterson and Mr. Graham the caretaker, and everyone had stopped making fun of us for being Italian behind our backs.
I didn't mind that we were different from then on. In fact, I began to enjoy it.

After my father had left for work, my mother would make real Italian coffee. Mr. Fazzi would supply the beans, and she'd grind them herself in one of those wooden boxes with a twisting handle on top. The smell was so delicious that you wanted to bury your face in it. Then she'd brew one of those Italian pots of coffee on the stove, pour us each a small bowl of it, add a splash of milk, and add some toast squares. That was our breakfast. I mean, did any other youngsters in the North East get to begin their school days like that?

My mother was a great woman. She was often surprising and delighting us with her recipes, which she had memorized. When we kids were around, she was always cheerful and smiling. She was always wanting us to see and do things that she couldn't.

But every now and then, the old agony would return. For example, while I was playing soldiers with the broom, I charged and destroyed her pastel pink chandelier in the living room, one of the few things she'd brought with her from Italy that hadn't been stolen or pawned. It was the first and last time I was afraid of my mother. She wasn't just furious; she was enraged.

But as soon as the wrath subsided, she burst into tears and embraced me in her arms.
This is perhaps a good time to tell that my mother tried again to take me back to Italy, this time with some advance notice and during a school holiday.
I was maybe seven or eight years old.

The only parts of the journey I recall are using a toilet on the train that emptied directly onto the tracks - dubbed "the loudest toilet in the world" - and being paralyzed with fear when we had to carry our suitcases across these narrow, wobbly planks onto the cross-channel ferry at Dover. I was convinced that we were both going to die. I'm not sure how my mum finally convinced me to join her.

Italy, on the other hand, was a revelation.

The station we arrived at, Roma Termini, was a brand-new modern marvel with a massive atrium and cantilevered ceiling that was unlike anything I'd ever seen before.

The Italian trains, which were diesel rather than steam and painted in the most magnificent reds, oranges, and greens, astounded me even more. And when we stepped off the train, the terminal smelled like coffee and fresh bread, and there wasn't a single item of rubbish in sight. In fact, nothing could blow around because there was no gale coming in from the North Sea. And it wasn't spitting on it. And I felt something strange on my face, something I'd never felt before... heat. Because of the sun.

I felt as if I had arrived in paradise.

I was astounded by how she lived. I can still see the delicate light blue and gold silk drapes and the kitchen, which featured a big table for cutting and preparing all of this fresh and colorful-looking food. Grape vines were spontaneously growing in ceramic pots on the balcony, spilling over the edge and climbing up the wooden latticework, producing a canopy of shadow.

That night, we were served the most delectable feast of pasta, fish, meats, and cheeses I'd ever had, and I got to sit at a special children's table with Julianna and my other Italian cousins. They gave me a small glass of red wine. And for the first time, the magnitude of what my mother had sacrificed for my father - for all of us - began to set in.

If my mother was the family's soul, my father was its backbone. Getting even a smidgeon of emotion from him was like getting blood from a stone. He mumbled. He grumbled. He occasionally yelled. He said very little most of the time. When he spoke to me, he generally said, 'Oy, you! 'Stop!' or 'Oy, you!' Gerrover has arrived!'

For years, I assumed my name was 'Hugh'.

He wasn't cruel in any way. He just didn't want to be perceived as weak. And that wasn't simply a machismo issue. Discipline is everything when you're a sergeant. If you can't keep your guys in line, someone will be killed sooner or later.

When I was approximately ten years old, I had my first inkling of what my father had gone through during the war on a Saturday afternoon. Back then, one of my favorite things to do was build Airfix model aircraft, and on that particular day, I was putting the finishing touches on an American P-38 Lightning twin-engined fighter bomber (dubbed 'The Fork-Tailed Devil' by the Germans). My father had never shown any interest in my works before, but when he returned from his club and saw the P-38, he stopped, grinned, and exclaimed, 'That's the most beautiful plane in the world.'

Which surprised me because he never said anything at all.
'What's the deal, Dad?'
'It saved our lives,' he explained.
That was the end of it. I was anticipating a tale, but discussing the war was just not cool. It took another twenty years for me to receive an explanation.

When I got home from school one afternoon, there was a massive cloud of black smoke pouring out over the top of the house, and I was like, "What the hell is that?" So, me and a couple of the other Big ones dashed to the source, which turned out to be a railway line that ran right behind our street and was separated from our back garden by only a little fence. This inspired us to invent an amazingly enjoyable new game, which the Little ones quickly joined in on. 'Steam train chicken' was the name of the game. As you can probably guess, this entailed us standing on the track waiting for a train while listening to the driver blow his whistle and yell every curse word he could think of at us, and seeing who could hold their nerve the longest before jumping out of the way.

In other words, the closer you were to a horrifyingly violent death, the better your chances of winning, which looked like a perfectly legitimate gamble to our kids.

Anyway, this game carried on for weeks, giving us with infinite hours of amusement until one day my father glanced out his bedroom window and observed what was going on.

Later that night, one of my friends' fathers arrived at my house, enraged, demanding to know why his son had been assaulted with a stick. But when my father recounted that he'd been caught playing chicken with a steam locomotive, the other parent became very quiet and said, 'Well, I'm sorry for doubting you, Alan. Please give him another good fucking hiding from me if you find him doing that again.

3. A Ruff Business

Warren Young knew I was a Catholic in a Church of England and Catholic Scout Troop while I was in the Sea Scouts, but then again, so did he. In the North East, we were dubbed "left footers."
He'd staged the Dunston Scout Gang Shows and had heard me sing, so he invited me to join The St. Joseph's Church Choir. I wasn't interested until he said I'd get paid one shilling and sixpence every week.

'I'd love to,' I replied.
And God had nothing to do with it; it was a business transaction.
On Wednesday night, he took me to choir practice, where there were approximately sixteen kids my age and older, as well as around twenty adults.
He requested me to sing a hymn for him and handed me a hymnal. When I looked closer, I noticed it was written in Latin. Goodbye, a shilling and sixpence.
I expressed my confusion, and he smiled and answered, 'Neither does anyone else.'
Then he handed me one that was phonetically written; ahh, this was much better.
This made you sound so saintly, Dominus vobiscum and everything. Only public school boys and priests spoke Latin.
It wasn't a song that I first learnt, but rather a phrase taught to me by one of the older boys: Nil carborundum illegitimi.
Which translates roughly as 'Don't let the tyrants crush you down.' A valuable life lesson.

Returning to choir practice, I performed "Oh Come, All Ye Faithful," and the choirmaster must have been impressed because he handed me a hassock or cassock, which made you even holy when you put it on. I only required the wings.

I was ready for my first engagement after about two weeks of practice: the 11:00 a.m. one-hour mass on the following Sunday.
To me, the Catholic mass was the most intricate means of worshiping a deity I had ever seen. When the priest spoke, the audience

responded in monotone drones. It was devoid of joy, and no one appeared to be content. God, on the other hand, isn't that amusing!

Then there were the altar boys, who moved around the stage, er, altar, dusting and polishing various items. With a silver chain, the priest drew out this container and tilted it from side to side, back and forth, with this foul-smelling smoke flowing out of it. It appeared to me to be voodoo, but money talks, and nonsense is king. Then we sang something that I thought was a bit of a relief, sort of like a commercial break. The priest then gathered his posse from the altar and marched down the aisle, pouring holy water on everyone. I tried using holy water to remove a food stain from my cassock once and it didn't work, so there you have it.

They returned to the stage, and Pop Gunning produced the box of crackers. Great, a tea break, I thought. Unfortunately, he lifted one of them up to the skies, muttered something extremely holy, and broke it into pieces, after which everyone in the audience came up for a piece and we sang while they ate. It took a while, but it helped pass the time... I was dizzy with boredom, and it had to end soon. I lost track of how many times they stood up, sat down, kneeled down, and stood up again. It was quite exhausting.

Pop stepped onto the pulpit sometime in the midst of the chaos to preach, asking us all to be nice and not to succumb to the temptation of eating meat on Friday, except spam because it wasn't real meat. He told us that God's anger was being poured out on us, and that the worse you were on Earth, the longer you would be in this place known as purgatory before being admitted to Heaven. He concluded by claiming that God loved us all, but he never mentioned the Holy Spirit. I think it's because being a ghost up there isn't particularly unusual. Then he returned to the altar, poured himself a glass of wine, and finished it all. He'd previously done the eight and nine o'clock masses and was still on his feet.

Pop and his gang exited the stage with us singing at full blast, yet no one clapped, which I thought was unfair. He was quite good in my opinion.

My mother was present, and she was overjoyed. She said I was the best singer there, as mothers are wont to do. However, during practice two weeks later, the choirmaster announced to the entire choir that I would be Head Choir Boy and handed me a golden belt to wear around my neck.

That's a lot of responsibility for someone who has no idea what the hell happened in a crowd, I thought. I simply followed everyone else, and now I'd have to sing solo every now and then. I knew I wasn't prepared.

The Head Choir Boys were said to have received two shillings and sixpence. Wow, a raise and a promotion in the name of God. However, there was a cost to pay. After practice, the deposed Head Choir Boy was waiting for me outside the church, and he was a big jerk. There is nothing scarier than an ex-Head Choir Boy whose voice has shattered. He jumped me as soon as I walked out the door and was systematically trying to knock the shit out of me when the choirmaster came out, booted him in the arse, pulled him off, and informed him that knocking the shit out of people is strictly forbidden on holy land (tell the Crusaders).

My proudest moment as a choir boy occurred at Christmas Eve midnight mass in 1960. I sung 'Silent Night' by myself. The church's lights were turned off, and it was only lit by candlelight. It was truly a lovely location to be. My mother appeared again, and she sobbed. It was very magical. There was no applause, but there was plenty of sighing and ahhing.
Not all of Warren Young's ideas ended happily.

But I was a teenager now, ready for anything - something Warren Young plainly admired in me - and I was probably feeling a little tough after beating the robber at the dairy. So I was one of the few morons who raised their hands to offer to join our team, despite the fact that I'd never worn boxing gloves in my life.

A tough training regimen ensued... consisting of only one practice round. Oh, and our troop only had two pairs of gloves, and the ones I got were bigger than my head, so I had to pack them with newspaper to keep them from flying off when I tried to jab. Even after stuffing them with newspaper, they still felt unsteady and loose - and by the conclusion of the round, I hadn't landed a single punch. But it was too late to back out by then.

When it was time for me to enter the ring, I could scarcely move my legs. I was terrified by the entire scene. The cords. The sound of the bell. Because of the cigarette smoke hanging from the ceiling, the church hall lights up a murky moon color. I had no notion why the first-aid man had a bucket in his hand. It was a devilish image.
Then I locked my gaze on my adversary.

He was four years my senior, five feet eight inches tall, and appeared to be on work release from prison. And, of course, he was dressed appropriately, with black shorts, boxing shoes, and gloves of the appropriate size, whereas I was dressed in my little school shorts, plimsolls, and gloves stuffed with newspaper. I've had a good life, I reasoned. At the very least, I'll go down swinging...

Looking back, it's difficult to believe that I became a teenager in 1960, of all years - the start of the greatest decade in history. I mean, consider the timing. My adolescent years would have been the same as every other generation of Geordies since before WWII if I had been born just a few years earlier. All music hall songs like 'Keep Yer Feet Still, Geordie Hinny' and 'Blaydon Races', no sex before marriage, and BBC variety shows. Instead, I was going to be treated to The Beatles, miniskirts, women's liberation, E-Type Jags, and moon missions. To be fair, we also had to deal with the Cold War and the ever-present prospect of nuclear war.

Even before the 1960s, you could sense a shift in the atmosphere of the country. The terrible poverty of the postwar period abruptly ceased, and a fresh, unexpected emotion took its place...

Optimism.

My life was transformed when I was cast as a child actress on Tyne Tees Television, where I appeared in various aspects of the weekly One O'Clock Show. My biggest role was in a future drama called In the Year 2000, and my one and only line was, 'Daddy, what's a cold?' - because colds were meant to be extinct by then. That's how wide-eyed and innocent we were...

My schoolwork began to suffer as soon as I became a teenager. I'd been at the top of the 'A' class for years. Then they developed a 'X' class to keep the top 'A' students from growing bored, and I topped that as well. But then I lost interest and dropped from No. 1 to No. 6... and my schooling was pretty much a lost cause after that. The culprit is music.

It didn't help that the school was overcrowded, with forty-eight students to a class, which meant the teachers spent more time keeping the peace than helping us learn. Or that secondary-modern students almost never went on to study A levels in the first place - you were on your own at the age of fifteen, with no reason to try harder.

If you can believe it, I even got into some trouble with the Sea Scouts.
The problem began with a 'field exam' that I had to pass in order to achieve the highest Sea Scout level of first class. This entailed me and another Scout, my best friend George Beveridge, traveling to a campground in County Durham called Beamish, where we were meant to trap and roast a wood pigeon according to a set of very particular instructions. We had from Friday afternoon after school until Sunday afternoon to complete this task, and we had to walk the seven miles or so from Dunston to Beamish because taking the bus or hitching a ride disqualified you.

So off we went in the wonderful sunshine - just joking, it was raining - and when we eventually arrived, we had to spend an unpleasant hour pitching our tent in the dark.
We didn't have a sleeping bag because they were way too expensive back then, so we had to make do with blankets fastened together with safety pins. And it was terribly cold and damp, and we hadn't brought enough food, but we were so exhausted that we fell asleep.

The next morning, we built our pigeon trap out of leaves, string, and twigs, with a door held open by another twig and a piece of bread inside as bait. When a hungry wood pigeon wandered in for a nibble, you would take out the twig, trapping the bird so you could wring its neck. Cooking the creature was a separate operation that included building a 'mud oven' in a riverbank. But we weren't going to waste time worrying about that until we'd caught our bird.

So we built the trap, set it up, and then sat back and watched.

We didn't realize it until it was mid-afternoon. We were starting to wonder why any wood pigeon in their right mind would choose to reside at a campsite where hungry Sea Scouts in shorts kept showing up to build wood pigeon traps.

We were still out of luck by four o'clock, and we were beginning to worry since an examiner would be arriving at noon the next day to look at our trap and sample our wood pigeon. And we were both adamant about becoming first-rate Sea Scouts. So we decided to travel to the nearest sign of civilisation, which turned out to be an old colliery town called Stanley, and see if we could get any assistance.

A poulterer's shop - similar to a butcher's shop, but only dealing in poultry and game - was conveniently located on Stanley's main thoroughfare. So we went in and asked the farmer-looking guy behind the desk in a flat cap how much a wood pigeon would cost. He informed us the price, we checked to see if we had enough money between us, and we did, so we decided to buy one right then and there.

We set about preparing the bird we'd 'caught' at the poulterer's store after a full night's sleep, making careful to follow the directions in the Sea Scout handbook to the letter.
We had to first remove its head, which was not an easy task. Then it walked away. Then we went down to the riverbank that ran through the campsite, named Beamish Burn, and dug two holes in the mud, one above the other. We built a fire in the bottom hole with chunks of wood and kindling, and we placed our wood pigeon in the upper one. Then we filled the top hole with mud, essentially making a

temporary clay oven. After approximately two to three hours of cooking, we got our billycans out and filled them with carrots, potatoes, and water, then cooked them over the fire. Our supper was almost ready to be served at this point.

Finally, the examiner arrived to grade our work.
It was a watershed moment. We'd officially become first-class Sea Scouts if he gave us the thumbs up. We'd have attained the height of Scouting success.

We returned to Dunston with knots in our bellies and a sense of failure. I despised the thought of disappointing Warren Young after everything he'd done for me. And I didn't want a dishonourable discharge from the Sea Scouts on my record when it came time to look for work. Who the fuck ever gets kicked out of the Sea Scouts? I could already hear my father's voice in my brain saying, 'You'll end up cleaning the roads!'

We had to go to our next troop meeting to explain ourselves to our Commodore, a retired naval captain in his seventies who resided in a room above a pub in Birtley for some unknown reason.
But the weird thing was... he didn't appear to mind.

Neither did Warren Young.
'Don't worry, lads, no one in the history of that test has ever caught a wood pigeon,' he told us. 'You're the first ones who at least showed a bit of initiative. We're always telling you to be prepared . . . and you were. I mean, aye, you should have been honest with the examiner . . . he's going to need a fair bit of dental work. But as I said to him myself, a Sea Scout can't learn without making mistakes!'
George and I just stood there in silence. Surely, we weren't going to get off this easily?
'So, er . . . we won't be dishonourably discharged, then?' ventured George.
'No, of course not!' snorted Warren Young. 'The examiner was just very cross.'
'So . . . we'll be, er . . . honourably discharged?' I asked.

'Noooo, no, no, no, no,' said Warren Young, laughing. 'We wouldn't discharge a Sea Scout over something as silly as that! And I think you've learned your lesson, right lads?'
We both nodded vigorously.
'Good,' said Warren Young, suddenly growing serious, 'because the decision's been made to put on another Gang Show – and I'm going to be needing both of your services . . .'

Warren Young did me his last and most important favor a few weeks later.

I knew he worked as a draughtsman at C. A. Parsons & Co., which was located over the river on Shields Road in Heaton. It was a vast complex, covering a hundred acres, with a railway terminus nearby and rails flowing directly into the factory buildings. The only way to truly understand its size was to see it for oneself. It's what people meant when they said Britain was the "world's workshop."

I'd always imagined that getting any kind of employment there would be impossible. It was well known that they only accepted about sixty apprentices a year from all across the North East, so the only way to get in was to be the finest of the best.

But Warren Young demanded that I apply, and he promised to put in a good word for me.
'Brian, son, you might not have gotten into grammar school, but you're a bright lad, full of energy, a hard worker, and, most importantly, you're always willing to try new things, whether it's stepping into a boxing ring, catching a wood pigeon, or dressing up as a Beverley Sister at the Gang Show. And don't worry... I won't include any of that in your reference letter.'

So I heeded his advise and applied, expecting to hear nothing back. Then I was invited in for an interview... and a few weeks later, a letter arrived that made my mother cry.

I'd been invited to become a Parsons apprentice, which meant five years of technical school and on-the-job training, followed by a union-protected job for life - as long as I didn't screw anything up.

Even my grandfather was overjoyed. Or, at the very least, when I told him the news, he grunted a little more enthusiastically than normal.

4. Crashes and Fires

It was summer 1966, and we were going down the A1 to Dover for our first overseas vacation, to my Italian side of the family's home in Frascati, near Rome. We are George Beveridge, Robert Conlin, and myself. England was leading Germany 4-2 in the World Cup at Wembley Stadium. What a day! Every German car we spotted received a two-finger salute. This was the life: three nineteen-year-old men in a brand-new Renault 4 - Rob Conlin's (he was an only kid, lucky git). We were going where our fathers had gone twenty years before, but we weren't going to be fired at.

We boarded the ferry in Dover, and the vehicles were incredible: Aston Martin 4s and 5s, Bentley Continentals, Facel Vegas, Ferraris, and even a Gullwing Mercedes, all on one ship. We couldn't believe there were so many wealthy individuals in the globe.

This was a moment when you were really pleased to be British. Honest. The Beatles and The Stones ruled the world, and Minis were everywhere, though in Italy they were built under license and called Innocenti. Norton, Triumph, BSA, Ariel, and James dominated the roost.

We were off. The ferry departed, and for the first time in my life, I saw what all the excitement was about with the White Cliffs of Dover. The drive through France, Switzerland, Northern Italy, and finally on the well-named Autostrada Sud to Frascati was simply breathtaking. We had a terrific time and quickly discovered that vehicles were important to the Italians. Alfas, Giuliettas, and Lancias. They were unusual.

We had no idea what was about to happen to us when we left after two wonderful weeks. The family piled cardboard boxes full of wine, hams, and salamis on us. We were suffocated. We left late as usual, and got lost a few times trying to find the road out of Frascati.

After driving all night, Robert Conlin was exhausted by 4 a.m. He wouldn't let George or myself assist him drive, in case 'we ruined the gears'. That's exactly what he said, I swear. So we slept as much as we could in the automobile. We were approximately a third of the way through France, on the feared N7 autoroute, which is notorious in motoring circles for death and damage. We had to travel to Calais for the boat or we'd be late for work in Newcastle on Monday. The day was Saturday, and the ferry ticket stated a departure time of 4.30 p.m. We'd be fine if we just kept traveling and stopped solely for gas.

We volunteered our driving services because Rob didn't seem good, but we were rebuffed yet again. 'Hey, Brian, how about a swap?' suggested George Beveridge. 'I'm tired of sitting in the back.' The back looked like a mobile grocer's, but it was my turn, so we switched. That was the best trade I'd ever done in my life.

One hour later, on the N7, a family of four was having a picnic by the side of the road in their Peugeot Estate. We'd just passed a car full of English nurses and waved to each other. Rob Conlin fell asleep at the wheel while driving at 70 mph, and before we could intervene, he collided with a Peugeot. Everything became black and white; I unexpectedly grew deaf; and it was all in slow motion: HOLY SHIT, is this thing ever going to stop rolling? According to witnesses, it went over seven times. The car's roof had been flattened to the door handle level. There was perfect quiet.

Then the screaming began. Rob Conlin was the screamer: the steering wheel had collapsed and the ignition key had gone through his ribcage. George had been thrown out of the front seat and onto a field. I was entrapped. This vehicle was rear-engined. There was no way out. I took long breaths and looked for blood. That is not possible. Ooh, you jammy git, I thought. The horrible dreadful French sirens were getting closer. Voices surrounded the automobile, English voices, girls' voices, nurses' voices. I sat and waited for help, but they had no idea I was there. They couldn't see me.

I must admit that I was a little concerned because the automobile was on its side, petrol was gushing everywhere, and the engine was hot. I started yelling, but subsequently learned that everyone was looking after Rob or in the field with George, who had suffered horrific injuries.

I decided to try to escape through the engine bay, stupid bugger. I yanked the seat away - not difficult in a 1960s Renault - put my hand in, and soon scorched myself. I yelled, 'OOYAH!' Just then, a pompier saw me and yelled, 'Cet git anglais entre l'auto est FUCKAYED!' (I think.)

They got me out and laid me down. The enormity of the exchange I conducted with George was beginning to sink in. My best friend was on a stretcher, seeming dead, being carried into an ambulance. Oh, George, don't die...

I couldn't understand why everyone was staring at me so strangely. I'd just survived a huge prang, and they were looking at me as if it was my fault. When the cop questioned if we'd been drinking, I realized I'd been saturated in Italy's finest wine. The only reason we weren't done was because I pointed out that all of the corks were still in the bottle necks. That's when the aching in my chest began. So I hadn't gotten away with it; it was an inside job resulting in three broken ribs.

I was placed in a village B&B. They were quite friendly to me. The others were in the hospital; I'll never forget that night. I knew I was alive, but I didn't know if George was. The next day, I went to the hospital. The boys were still alive. It was a little battered, but that didn't matter. We had no money, so all we cared about was getting out of there. George had stitches all over his face and was still bleeding. We achieved this by rubbing some of his blood on my face, jumping into bed, and pretending to be George, while George dressed in a cupboard with Rob's help. We then went to the train station to board a train to Paris, with hospital officials hounding us to settle the cost.

A nice man from the British Embassy had gotten us tickets to England on the boat train, but just to London. We had no money for food, and we were starving. After trekking across London with our stuff in cardboard boxes, we got three tickets home by promising to repay the people who had lent us the money within a month.

Finally, on Sunday afternoon, we arrived in Newcastle. What must we have looked like, George as a juvenile Frankenstein and me with blood all over my pants? That's when Rob Conlin pulled out his cash and announced he was taking a cab home. The bugger has money all the time! George and I dragged ourselves four kilometers to Dunston, our hometown.

I arrived at C. A. Parsons & Co. Ltd at 7.25 a.m. on Monday morning, fractured ribs and all. George went to the hospital to get more glass out of his face. He still has a fragment in his mind.
After my apprenticeship ended, Parsons called and offered me a permanent position.

I was a true grown-up now.
And no, I didn't like the sound of that either.

Part Two
5. Oops

New Year's Eve, 1966.

I'm young, single, and unmarried, and things couldn't be better.
For starters, I've moved on from Section 5, and I'm now the singer of a far better band with a considerably more sensible name. Okay, that last bit isn't true. We're called The Gobi Desert Kanoe Klub, which we saw written on a novelty T-shirt sold in the back of the New Musical Express, next to an offer for stick-on sideburns... which we ordered without thinking to verify the color. Let's just say that I walk on stage with maracas and a tambourine. Oh, and we don't do 'gigs'. We do 'happenings' and, even better, 'love-ins'.

Did I mention I've got a new girlfriend? Yes, and she's a beauty. Flaming red hair. Blue eyes. Carol is her name, and we can't take our hands off each other.
And now, just before midnight, we're at the home of The Gobi Desert Kanoe Klub's rhythm guitarist, Dave Yarwood, a man bravely sporting a bowl cut matched with a floral blouse and tight white leggings.

Dave, like everyone else in the room that night, is that most amazing and improbable of creatures: a hippie in Newcastle. In the North East in 1966, there were hundreds, if not thousands, of us. Our God is the sweet-voiced Scott McKenzie, and our song is 'San Francisco,' despite the fact that San Francisco is a very, very long way from Dave's house here on Scotswood Road.

Now, New Year's Eve - or Old Year's Night, as some call it - is a major deal in Newcastle, and not only because Geordies will embrace any excuse for a piss-up. When the clock strikes midnight, every ship on the Tyne blasts its horn, and the entire city vibrates to this spooky, stirring sound, which carries for miles through the fog and rain. Then it's time for 'first-footing,' when the first person to enter a house on 1 January brings a lump of coal for good luck and is greeted on the other side with a glass of whisky and a rousing chorus of 'Auld Lang Syne'... unless the first-footer is a woman or a redhead, in which case a curse will befall you for the next twelve months. Given the abundance of lasses and gingers in these parts, it's an odd superstition - but don't blame me, I'm half Italian, and I had nothing to do with it.

To this day, neither Carol nor I can recall a single detail between the clock hitting midnight and our waking up in each other's arms the next morning on Dave's living room floor.

All I know for sure is that we both got quite intoxicated...
And one of us became really pregnant.
Knocking up your girlfriend at the age of nineteen while working full-time in a factory was hardly performance enhancing in the battle to gain fame and money as a rock'n'roll singer.

It's not that I regret it. You won't be sorry. My darling Joanne, who was born nine months later, has provided me more joy and love than I could ever put into words.

But my timing could have been better.
It couldn't have been much worse.

For aspiring rock'n'roll musicians, Britain in early 1967 was about as good as it could get. It was like being a Christopher Columbus-era explorer in Portugal. Or a Renaissance-era painter in Italy. When you consider what was going on at the time, it's simply mind-boggling. The Rolling Stones had recently issued a double A-side of "Let's Spend the Night Together" and "Ruby Tuesday." The Beatles' Sgt. Pepper's Lonely Hearts Club Band was about to be released, as was Jimi Hendrix's Are You Experienced and The Kinks' single "Waterloo Sunset." The BBC would then introduce Radio One a few months later.

Radio One alone would be a game changer. Before it went on the air, all BBC Radio offered was the dreadful Light Programme or, even worse, the Home Service, with its shipping forecasts that seemed to go on for days at a time, describing every last gust of wind and drop of rain in places only a handful of fishermen knew existed.

'Holmsgarth, northwest, two to four... mostly fair, occasionally poor... Lochmaddy, intermittent light rain falling gently...'

Despite this, they proceeded to play 'Flowers in the Rain' by The Move - the first song ever played on Radio One. Because I couldn't tear myself away from the Rediffusion radio in the kitchen, I missed a quarter-hour's pay that morning.
When I arrived to work, all I could think about was coming home to listen to it again.

To be fair, even before I became an unintentional father, I felt as if the 1960s were slipping away from me. After all, my position at Parsons wasn't just a nine-to-five. Even after it was told to me that working the 9 p.m. to 7.30 a.m. shift meant double money and a four-day week, I was upset. But I couldn't care less about the extra cash, even though I desperately needed it. I really wanted to go out and play with the band at night.

I recall my first night shift vividly. I was walking to the factory gate with two other trainees when I witnessed the most spectacular sunset. Now, for all the crap I give the North East about its weather, I can tell you, hand on heart, that it has the best sunsets in the world. Because you're so far north that it never gets completely dark, the wind becomes God's paintbrush, and the rain clouds His palette, and the sky just explodes into these magnificent swirls of pinks, oranges, and reds, especially in summer.

My dissatisfaction was exacerbated by the fact that I'd begun seeing a lot of big-name artists, giving me a taste of the kind of life I could have if I ever became a professional singer.

The first movie I recall seeing was at Newcastle's Odeon Cinema on Pilgrim Street. Admission was free since it was sponsored by a cigarette manufacturer, which was fine back then because cigarettes were healthy - at least, according to the doctors who approved them. Julie London was the headliner. I remember them handing us each a pack of twenty at the door, which felt like Christmas had arrived early for me and my companion, George Beveridge. We usually had to buy them in packs of ten because we were so broke. Aside from the main attraction, there was a lineup of bands who each performed two songs. The Bachelors, The Fourmost, and finally The Pretty Things took the stage and nearly blew the doors off with "Don't Bring Me Down."

I would have traded places with any of those guys on stage, especially The Pretty Things.
The legendary Cockney music manager Mike Jeffery's Club a'Gogo was one of the reasons the best acts all came to Newcastle. Because Jeffery had engaged a superb young vocalist named Eric Burdon to head the house band, it quickly became the North East's answer to the Marquee in London.
The band in question was, of course, The Animals.

Everyone had a good time at the Club a'Gogo. The Stones. The band The Who. Tina and Ike Turner. Wolf Howlin'. The Animals even dedicated a song to the location, which was issued as the B-side to "Don't Let Me Be Misunderstood." That's how hot it was. However, there were numerous more thriving venues in town. There was La Dolce Vita, The Downbeat, Change Is, The Oxford, The Majestic, The Cavendish, and, of course, The Mayfair, which featured a spectacular spinning stage.

I was so taken with that song that we tried to cover it in The Gobi Desert Kanoe Klub...
However, in the first verse, we ran out of talent.

I knew he was coming to town the instant I heard his name. Even before anyone had heard his music, the person had gone viral, with the Record Mirror publishing a profile of him dubbed "Mr. Phenomenon." Then came Are You Experienced, with the opening track, 'Foxy Lady,' believed to be about Roger Daltrey's girlfriend, and I remember listening to it and thinking, what the fuck is this? It was as if the person had beamed himself in from another realm... bringing with him a whole new set of musical frequencies.

Louder ones

Of course, I didn't have enough money to buy a ticket. It didn't matter since they were gone in an instant. So I did what any other enterprising young man would do in the same situation. When the bouncers weren't looking, I crawled in beneath the admissions box on my hands and knees.
I was already running up the stairs and into the crowd when someone noticed me.

The venue was completely full. We're talking about doubling or triple capacity. You could hardly breathe. I've now learned that at the same gig was Gordon Sumner, a.k.a. Sting, who was only fifteen years old at the time. An even younger James Bradford, a.k.a. Jimmy Nail, who had not yet turned thirteen, was also present. I should certainly point out that the Club a'Gogo had two rooms. One was labeled 'The Young Set' because it catered to people under the age of 18, and the other was labeled 'The Jazz Lounge' because it catered to an older, more sophisticated population. We were in The Young Set on this night because the event in the Jazz Lounge didn't start until the horrible hour of 2 a.m.

Even Sting recalls some commotion as management attempted to locate the intruder. ('That was you?!' he exclaimed when I informed him years later.) But I found a space near the rear where I could stand quietly and listen. And all I could do was listen since I couldn't see anything except a headband, the top of a guitar, and some ribbon. But then Hendrix swung his guitar and got it trapped in the artificial ceiling - not difficult in such a tremendously cramped environment. Most guitarists would have halted the act, but he just kept playing it while it hung there.
If memory serves, with his teeth at one point.

The place got totally insane.
The world will never see another Hendrix. Just the guy's aura. The charisma. Words cannot do him justice. To be honest, the sound was terrible. I mean, really horrible. I couldn't even see a road crew. There was only Mitch Mitchell on drums and Noel Redding on bass. There was no mixing desk, no sound guy, just the three boys on stage and this incredible, completely overwhelming roar, everything cranked up to its maximum, fuses flashing, sparks flying, the air

fizzing and crackling with high-voltage current. The truth is that Jimi Hendrix's genius fingers fashioned and sculpted the entire thing. Through his guitar, he let his soul out.

The band may have dubbed themselves an experience, but they were truly an assault. When you came out, you knew the world had changed and that you had changed. I notice the similar effect when Angus Young goes free, utterly lost in himself and utilizing the guitar to express himself.
Needless to say, I was immediately hooked.

My ears were still ringing from the Hendrix show when The Gobi Desert Kanoe Klub got together.
Yours truly on vocals, Dave Yarwood of the New Year's Eve party renown on guitar, and another really decent guitarist named Ken Brown round out the lineup. (I'd met Ken at Parsons; he had long hair and a moustache, and later fell for Carol's sister, Jen, finally becoming my brother-in-law.) Meanwhile, on bass was my old pal Steve Chance, and on drums was a young man with the fantastic Monte Carlo name of Fred Smith.

There's a photo someplace of us all sitting on the back steps of Dave's house, trying to seem cool.
Ken had intended us to be called Half Past Thirteen, if I recall right. But we all thought that was a bad idea.

We had enormous ideas, of course. But our shaky covers of John Mayall & The Bluesbreakers and the Paul Butterfield Blues Band - my little 10-Watt Watkins P.A. system utterly drowned out by Dave and Ken's guitars - were never going to get us far.
But the band did offer me with one of the most important rites of passage in any musician's career.
I was at my parents' house at the time, looking out the front window. The dreadful shrieking began first. Then came the loud clatter. Then, in a swirl of exhaust smoke, an Austin J2 van with the words 'Gobi Desert Kanoe Klub' on the side arrived.

For all the talk of us performing 'love-ins' and 'happenings' - there was only ever one love-in, an outdoor event put on by Newcastle

University students to collect money for 'rag week' - the only places that would book us were the grimmest of North East pubs. Working men's clubs, which had not yet gained their absolute domination of the 1970s, just weren't mainstream enough. They preferred to book comedians, jugglers, and magicians.

'Can you not see anything from the charts?' When we were hired in certain locations, the audience would yell. Then we'd do another Paul Butterfield number, and everybody who wasn't flipping their tab ends at us in disgust would just leave.

Even less successful was our foray into 'events,' which amounted to one booking from Steve Chance's uncle, who'd just opened the first motel in Northumberland, up the Roman road on the way to Carlisle, in the utter middle of nowhere. But what a lovely place.

And it was here that Steve Chance's uncle, the wannabe billionaire that he was, had decided to build his motel. Going where no Northumbrian had gone before was groundbreaking, because they didn't know what a motel was.

We didn't realize we'd be playing for a local fire department's Christmas party until we arrived - which was a miracle in and of itself given the state of the van. This meant the audience would be primarily made up of big males in their 40s and 50s, as well as their spouses, and they'd be eating into a cigarette ash-strewn buffet of ham and peas pudding sandwiches and pies while we played.

We huddled for an emergency rehearsal after our equipment was set up. Dave, Ken, and Steve tried to figure out the chords, I tried to remember the lyrics, and Smithy hammered down the rhythm. (This was 1968; you couldn't just open your music app and listen.) We stepped up on stage, still feeling completely unprepared, and did our best to get through the song. I was simply making stuff up throughout the verse, but the chorus was simple enough: Roy Wood wanted someone to 'run-and-get-the-fie-uh-bruh-gaade' because the girl he sat next to at school was so lovely. And the audience didn't care; they just wanted to sing along.

I'd never been so relieved in my life as we neared the finale.

We must have played it five times. Then some astute individual called up and requested "Penny Lane." It took a while for that one to sink in. Then I remembered the words about the fireman keeping his fire engine clean. But we had to try. You don't debate with a room full of irritated firemen.

I'm not sure if it was the firefighter gig, the fact that I was about to become a new dad, or our failure to get into the larger places where our type of music was played that destroyed us.

In any case, the van died around the same time as we did. I was travelling back to North Shields one night after leaving everyone off at their homes when I noticed blue lights behind me. Oh, sh*t. The cops had pulled me over. Which was a problem, not least since the van's brakes didn't function, so the only way to stop it was to put it into first gear with the pliers, while yanking up the handbrake and hoping it didn't cause some kind of catastrophic mechanical breakdown.

Then he noticed the tax disc... which was, of course, a Brown Ale label. Any van owned by anyone under the age of twenty-five in the North East had a Brown Ale label instead of a tax disc (or so I thought). It appeared as though Scottish & Newcastle Breweries had purposefully produced it nearly the same shape and size. 'I'm going to pretend I didn't see that,' stated the cop. 'And, to make both of our lives a little simpler, I'm not even going to ask if you have insurance, since I'm very confident I already know the answer to that question. But I'm going to insist on you following me - slowly - to the police station, where I'm going to take control of this van and put it out of its agony. 'On the scrap heap.'

My heart fell.

No transportation meant no gigs, which meant no band.
But the truth was that I had more important things to worry about.

Carol and I married on June 1, 1968, at which time she had a visible bulge. Everyone had attempted to convince us out of marrying. Carol's mother had offered to look after the baby. My father had constantly assuring me that I still had my entire life ahead of me and that I had no idea what I was getting myself into. But, like every other adolescent before me, I didn't listen. It just seemed proper to marry the girl I'd gotten pregnant with.

The service flew by. We were only kids. We had no notion how to act in such a situation. All I can say is that Dave Yarwood was the best man and that my mother created the wedding gown.

After the vows were exchanged, my father asked, 'You happy?'
'I'll be OK, Dad,' I murmured, but worry was written all over my face. How was this going to work? How was I going to manage a full-time job, extra half-shifts, a wife and a baby, and play in a rock'n'roll band? Of course, I knew the answer. I couldn't. Something had to give. And it wasn't going to be the job, the extra half-shifts, or caring for a wife and a baby.

The reception was held in a venue close to the chapel. My entire family, including my grandfather and grandmother, was present. Every woman got a sherry, and every man got a whisky. Then we sat down to this extremely inexpensive yet wonderful hot buffet. Because we were all half-cut, everyone was getting along like a house on fire by this point.

I ended up trying to cook and failing badly. On my wedding night.
When we returned to North Shields the next day, I moved into Carol's bedroom at her parents' house, a practice common among newlyweds at the time. It felt odd, especially when I came down for breakfast the next morning. Not to mention crowded, given that they had two other children in the house.

Looking back, I'm not sure how we did it.
Meanwhile, my musical career was stagnating. In fact, it was going backwards because I'd stopped gigging totally. The Gobi Desert Kanoe Klub was no more, and none of the bigger bands in town would hire a singer with a 10-watt P.A. system. For good reason. To

be heard over a rock band at a theatre or nightclub, or even one of the larger working men's clubs, you needed a much larger amp and a decent Shure microphone. But even with a hire-purchase agreement, that was much out of my price range.

Then Carol's father, Bill, did something remarkable that lifted a great burden off all of our shoulders. He had some insurance money from a work accident, so he acquired a close downstairs unit for £600 - 61 Chirton West View was the address, and he allowed us move there as tenants for close to nothing in rent. It was his first home. (He rented one from the council.)
I could have sobbed when he informed us.

Yes, the place was built in 1910, and there was moisture on the walls, and the toilet was outdoors, straight at the rear of the yard, in an outhouse so frigid that there was a hammer hanging on the wall to break the ice on frosty mornings. But at least we had a space to call our own. And it had a coal fire in the bedroom and another in the living room, so we could have heated the home if we'd had any money. However, a tiny bag of coal from the corner shop cost two shillings and seven pence and lasted only a couple of hours. So we elected to shiver and save our money for dinner instead.

Carol was not as enthusiastic about life as I was. She was only sixteen years old and should have been out having fun. But she had to stay at home to care for a newborn. Looking back, I feel terrible for her. But our little Joanne was a continual source of joy, as was her sister Kala when she arrived a few years later. You can't put into words how much love both of our daughters brought us. That's why I wouldn't alter a thing.

When I returned to my parents' house one night, I discovered my father on the street outside, red in the face, shouting in his loudest sergeant's voice at my sister Julie and some guy she was seeing. Julie was probably fifteen or sixteen at the time.

Julie was in floods of tears, and her lover was so terrified that he turned tail and escaped. But my father kept ranting, and I snapped. I felt like he was always yelling at someone, typically my mother, and it was embarrassing and needless. But, of course, the truth was that I, too, was stressed beyond the breaking point.

'Enough, Dad!' I screamed at him, almost as loudly as he did. 'What is this all about?'
But my father was in a rage. 'Don't talk to me like that, or I'll take your head off!' he yelled.
'I don't think so, Dad,' I replied. 'You touch me, and I'll -'

My father went after me like I was a ten-year-old boy. But I was a grown guy, powerful from all my industrial labor, and I was on a hair trigger. So I whacked him. It was more difficult than I had anticipated. And after he fell, I leapt on him and told him that if he ever bullied anyone in my family again, I wouldn't hold him accountable. He was flustered and frustrated, and I couldn't tell if he was pleased of me for sticking up for myself or horrified and appalled.

It didn't matter in the end. I felt so bad that I went back the next day to apologize.
I only got grunts in reply. But I guess he felt awful as well, because everything was good after that. But the shock of that jolted me awake and made me understand that I couldn't keep going like this, looking for a miracle.
It was past time for me to act.

6. A Horrible Shit Shower

The solution to my issues came from an odd source: a young man called Jimmy Shane, who ran into the light machine shop at Parsons one morning, overjoyed, since he'd just signed up for the Territorial Army, Britain's equivalent of the National Guard.

'All you have to dee is march aroond on a Wednesday, and every odd weekend you get to gan up the range and fire a gun!' he told me, speaking so quickly, I could barely understand him. 'And if you stick it oot for a year, they give you a £200 bounty!'
'What?' I said, barely able to believe what I thought I'd just heard.
'I said . . . all you have to dee is march aroond on a –'
'No, no, no – the last part.'
'If you stick it oot for a year, they'll give you a £200 bounty!'
Holy shit, I thought – this is it. This is how I can buy a bigger P.A. system! This is how I can get back on stage . . . but this time with a bigger, better band. (I also loved the idea of earning a 'bounty'.)
I ran down to the T.A. recruitment office that same day and filled out an application form. Then I was taken to a separate room for a rigorous medical exam.
Doctor: 'Name and address?'
Me: '61 Chirton West View, North Shields.'
Doctor: 'Is there anything wrong with you?'
Me: 'Well, er –'
Doctor: 'You're in.'

Now, I should add that there were several divisions you could join, but the parachute regiment - the one Jimmy Shane had signed up for - was the only one that paid you the nearly unfathomable sum of £200. For example, if you joined the engineers, you would be paid 'just' £125. Furthermore, in the paras, you were guaranteed an £8 extra for every time you jumped out of a plane - not that I ever imagined myself doing that. I mean, the British government didn't have any money at the time. And that was peacetime. And the North East. So the concept of sending men like me up on joyrides in the air seemed ridiculous. In my opinion, the paras would be a step up from the Sea Scouts. We'd put on our uniforms, go through some drills, maybe go on a camping trip, and by the end of the year, I'd be £200 richer, thank you very much.

The next thing I knew, I was reporting for duty after work in a drill hall in Gosforth, a wealthy area just north of Newcastle. I'd even convinced George Beveridge to accompany me. After hearing about the bounty, he didn't need much convincing.

As we reached the drill hall, I felt a shiver run down my spine as I heard command yells and marching feet. And a part of me was thinking, oh, fuck yeah. I mean, I was nervous, too, since the T.A. guys appeared to be tough guys, but when they took a break and started chatting to us, they couldn't have been nicer.

The drill sergeants were not the same. When they called out your name - or rather, screamed it in your face - it was almost always followed by, 'You awful shower of shit.'

The first thing I had to do was sign the Official Secrets Act, which seemed a bit much but also rather exciting.
Then I got my first order: 'YOU! YOU HORRIBLE SHOWER OF SHIT! GET YOUR FUCKIN' HAIR CUT!'

Oh, no. I'd forgotten you required a short back and sides to join the military. I should have remembered the footage of Elvis getting his head shaved and being taken to West Germany to sit on a tank. My hair was long and curly, and it looked great on stage. But it was useless to me without a PA system. And who was I to object if Jimi Hendrix had been a U.S. Marine?

I was given a used outfit that smelled of ancient battlefields and hookers, not to mention old stains. We were handed new boots, brand new and gleaming black, with khaki puttees, or leg-bindings, followed by the coveted crowning glory, my red beret. The only exception was the beret, which lacked wings. You have to earn them.

We were subsequently instructed to schedule two weeks of vacation from our jobs for Basic Training. This was another surprise for me. What the fuck was Basic Training all about? I was about to find out.

Basic training was held in Catterick Garrison, on the outskirts of the Yorkshire Dales.
The group of lads I was with had been put under the command of The Pig, a small, stout, and tremendously boisterous Glaswegian drill sergeant.

When The Pig shrieked an order, the word 'you' would exit his throat as 'YEEEEEEOOOWW!' - the same sound you'd make if someone tried to push a cheese grater up your rectum. And when The Pig marched us up and down the parade ground - which was pretty much all of the time - his 'lefts' would come out as 'EFFs!' and his 'rights' as 'HAIGHTs!' 'EFF-HAIGHT! EFF-HAIGHT! EFF-HAIGHT!'
Yes, The Pig's love of agony was renowned. As was his generosity in passing it around.

Our lodgings in Catterick were World War II-era Nissen huts, which were basically sheets of corrugated iron bent into half cylinders with a breeze block wall and a door at each end. There was a stove pipe for heating, but we didn't use it because we'd have to clean it out every night to pass The Pig's morning inspection - The Pig would drop a sixpence on your bedsheets, and if the coin didn't bounce, it meant you hadn't pulled the sheets tight enough, and you'd have to face his wrath.

Our days would begin at the crack of dawn, when The Pig would roam around slamming two trashcan lids together very near to our heads.
After that, it was breakfast at the Naafi - a.k.a. the canteen - followed by non-stop marches, drills, lectures on gun maintenance, then visits to the firing range till it was time to eat, then hit the sack. You'd be so tired by then that you'd fall asleep the second your head hit the pillow.

The firing range should have been the highlight. But we were too nervous about failing the test to have any pleasure. There were no telescopic sights or any of that nonsense. And the targets were around 200 to 300 yards away, with some as far away as 600 yards, and The Pig would be breathing down your neck, yelling things like,

'No, no, no! Not at all! 'Keep your hand steady!' just as you were ready to fire the trigger. I qualified as average, which means I missed as many as I hit - enough to pass the test.

The benefit of all the adversity was how completely you bonded with your fellow recruits.
Within a few days, I'd made fast friends with Jimmy Shane, the person who'd inspired me to join the T.A., as well as another kid named Jimmy Smith and a gigantic fella we simply knew as The Dane. But, of course, the more comfortable we became in each other's presence, the more we began to goof around...

Never a good idea in the military.
When we went out for parade one morning and The Pig was unable to be found, I decided to do my best impression of him in front of the men. I must have been doing a terrific job because the lads were laughing with laughter - until they suddenly stopped and stood to attention. I thought to myself, "Wow, I'm pretty good at this." Then I heard heavy breathing from behind me and a voice filled with open hatred. 'I despise you, Johnson, and I'm going to make your life miserable.'
Oh, shit... The Pig.

I was no longer alive.
He made me run around the parade grounds with my weapon held above my head until the morning parade was over.
We had a twenty-mile route march with full kit, then we returned to camp; the lads went to the Naafi, but not me. Sergeant Pig had other plans, such as going around the parade ground again with that fucking big rifle, which was becoming heavier. Following that, I cleaned up a massive coal bunker till he was satisfied. My arms were tired, and the PA system felt a long way away. Needless to say, slapping the monkey was out of the question for the next few days.

After completing Basic Training, I was essentially a part-time soldier. But, in order to be the entire parachute package, I had to leap out of a perfectly decent plane at 800-1,000 feet, which required us to attend parachute training school at RAF Abingdon in Oxfordshire.

There were around forty guys there, all wondering what they'd gotten themselves into. Laughter was way too loud, and swagger was bouncing off the walls, indicating that we were all terrified.

The absence of parade ground yelling is the first thing you notice when visiting a Royal Air Force post. Everyone was incredibly friendly and professional, and the sergeant that welcomed us was so adorable.

'Hello lads, I hope you had a pleasant journey; now follow me and I'll take you to your quarters so you may settle in. I'll be back in an hour to show you where you'll have lunch.'

This was fantastic. I liked this charming, polite sergeant, and then lunch was great. The canteen was much better than I had hoped. This is where the bomber crews ate breakfast after a night raid over enemy territory, magical stuff.

The food was really tasty. After dessert, the nice sergeant fella said, 'Right boys, we'll now walk to the lecture hall and explain you what the next two weeks of training will consist of and introduce you to your jump sergeants (masters).'

I had the impression that someone had just walked over my grave, but I chalked it up to an errant bowel movement. We entered the lecture auditorium, and there, with a sparkle in his eye, stood the feared Pig. Oh, no! I'm dead, and he must have read my mind because he gave me a minuscule nod.

He'd brought his friends this time, and they all seemed ready to get started on the jumping from a tremendous height thing. My aspirations of singing in a band in front of an adoring audience faded, as did visions of a long life. Nonetheless, I was determined to see it through.

The following morning began with the normal parade and inspection, followed by breakfast and instruction on how to fall from various heights. The sergeants would always cry 'GO!' directly in your ear, and when they did, you went.

Climbing The Tower was the most terrifying part. It was just an electric pylon, and as you got to the top, it shook with the wind. The fear element was sphincter-rattlingly disastrous. Then they wrapped a harness over your waist and shoulders, which was hooked to a cable. This was connected to a pulley, which when you jumped spun a two-foot square board, which served as your brake.

The jump sergeant was having the thrill of his life watching wide-eyed recruits pee their pants as they realized how high up they were. I attempted to be civil to him, and he grinned and said, 'GO!' so I did.

You must understand that at the start of this training, we were told that if you hesitated or refused to jump, you would be out of camp in thirty minutes, bags and all, so you couldn't tell anybody else about your anxiety.

That afternoon, we were told that our first genuine parachute jump would be the next morning. One youngster whooped and cheered, but we beat the crap out of him.
The next morning was a lovely blue-sky day. Nobody ate much breakfast. We waited in line for our parachutes, and as we strapped them over our crotch, waist, and shoulders, you questioned if yours was okay. We'd been warned about the dreaded 'roman candle,' which implies the chute won't open, and the tune we sung when inebriated was the ancient parachute rhyme.

'Right gentlemen, verify your reserve chute is properly set in position on your chest, and the red handle is facing up and if you lose the handle in any manner, we shall remove 10 shillings and sixpence out of your pay. 'Stay with me.'

I thought to myself, bollocks! All I needed was a public address system. This was never done by the Beatles or the Rolling Stones. They were driving about, shagging birds and getting high, but not quite as high as I was!

We followed the jump masters to our air conveyance. Like the Montgolfier brothers, it was a basket suspended from a balloon. 'This isn't a fucking balloon, it's a dirigible, and that bottom isn't a basket, it's a gondola,' exclaimed the sergeant major. You shall face my wrath if you call it anything else!'

I'm not sure what was going through my thoughts, but it looked like a white cross with a poppy on it. We were supposed to leap in five-person groups. I ranked fourth.
'All right, now it's your turn to follow me.'

And we succeeded. We walked into this basket, er, gondola, hanging on for dear life. Then it began to ascent, and the J.M. yelled, 'HOOK UP!' We attached our chutes to the static line. We climbed higher and higher. This was proper stuff, for God's sake. My arse was doing its best squirrel-nose impression. But the most terrifying aspect was the complete and utter silence. You could hear birds breaking the wind because it was so silent.

'Right, fellas, we've arrived at 800 feet. Follow my instructions to the letter.' There was a doorway that was always open. We were still holding on to the basket's rail for dear life.

'What are you holding that for, you'll all be jumping in a minute,' says the narrator.
That's when it hit me: screw the PA, screw the music, I want to live.
'Number one, go to the door, put your hand on the door, and GO!'
And he proceeded, one, two, three... 'Fourth, to the door, GO!'
And I did, and I dropped and kept falling until a large hand pulled me up and I was drifting down, laughing as I steered my chute. When I landed, it didn't hurt; it was an exhilarating feeling of relief, and I wanted to do it again because I'd just earned £8.
We performed one more for £16 that day.

To earn your parachutes, you had to accomplish seven jumps, two from a dirigible and five from an airplane, which was new and exciting.
We gathered in the hangar the next morning and were given our 60lb kit packs. These were linked to your right leg, and a fifteen-foot lanyard-type thing with a quick-release hook was attached to your waist strap. You had to let go of the bag, which hung from your

waist, once you had jumped and your chute was fully open. That is, your equipment was immediately beside you when you landed.

The problem was that these things began to oscillate, which means they swung like a pendulum and could severely mess with your genitalia. Furthermore, if you were terrified and threw it away, you'd be neck deep in shit from everyone who mattered. Basically, it was extremely risky for those beneath you.

The feeling of leaping out of an airplane is perplexing for both men and boys. You can hardly walk with 60lb strapped on your back, and the aircraft engines are making a lot of noise (this was my first trip on a plane). Climbing into the fuselage, locating the netting, determining which seat was yours. Checking to make sure your helmet was fastened; no grins, no jokes, just hard expressions on everyone's faces.

The plane takes off, slowly ascending. It was an old and tired Blackburn Beverley.
We form a circle, and then the jump master takes a stand. He lowers his gaze and raises both hands. That translates as 'stand up'. We do so and confront him.
'Hold on!'

We can't hear him, but we can see his forefinger crook.
'VERIFY EQUIPMENT!'

That implies you should double-check the straps on the man in front to make sure he's okay to go. Meanwhile, let's hope the person in front of you is doing the same. Then you're done. The red light is on, what am I doing here? I find myself in similar circumstances all the time. 'Dear Mrs. Johnson, please accept a bucket containing the remains of PVT Johnson.' Brian, put your thoughts aside.

The first man has left, thanks to the green light. You can't see anything until you come to the door, at which point you can see the earth.

I was gone a long way down and fast. For a few seconds, I was almost horizontal, and suddenly that glorious chute opened up, phew!

I completely forgot about the quick release. I let go, and my kit bag falls and hangs there, and we both fall. I land gently and pull into the chute. I made it (£24), so I'm safe.

We did four more, all equally amazing and terrifying, but I'd fucking done it.

7. Highway to . . . Nowhere

We arrived in Torquay, on the Devon coast, a month after 'All Because of You' entered the Top 10. The date was April 23, 1973, Easter Monday. The date stands out in my memories because it was one of those days when it looked like the universe was trying to tell me something.

Torquay is just about fifty miles from France, and we'd been told it has a near-tropical climate with palm trees lining the streets. And, being gullible Scots, we believed it, booked a B&B right on the seafront and packing our swimming trunks and suntan lotion.

We shared a room with four older men, and each of us slept in one of those small divan beds that you fall out of if you roll over in the middle of the night. The paint on the walls was chipping away. The sheets were made of a nylon that gives you electric shocks as you move. And, of course, there was no heat until you inserted 5p pieces into the room's meter, which we stopped doing after realizing 5p only earned you about five minutes of warmth. The heat simply escaped through the gaps surrounding the window frames.

We did, however, have a place to sleep. Back then, B&B proprietors were renowned for giving your room away before you arrived, especially if you arrived late.
Our landlady was not at all friendly.

'I lock the door at exactly midnight, so if you're not back by then, you're out of luck.' She said that a toaster and some bread will be made accessible at the crack of dawn for roughly twenty minutes.
'What if we don't make it?' So I inquired.
'You won't need it.'

The bus parked outside was the first thing we noticed when we pulled up. A massive American type from the early 1950s, featuring stainless-steel side panels and a bullet-shaped back end, rather than a regular bus. It was a Flxible Clipper, which I subsequently discovered had been manufactured for an Australian tour company, explaining why it was right-hand drive. I couldn't imagine that a car of that size and design had made it into the country.

'Who is it?'
Vic shrugged, 'Must be the backup band's. Support acts were frequently even poorer than us. So how could they afford such transportation?

When we arrived, the backup band in question was still on stage, with about fifteen minutes to go, so we ordered some drinks, sat at the bar, and listened.

The band was from Australia, and they had recently changed their name from Fraternity to Fang after a disastrous debut in the United Kingdom the previous year. I couldn't take my eyes off the lead singer, who was one of the most wild-looking animals I'd ever seen. Coconut bob. There is one tooth missing. Abraham Lincoln's beard. He appeared to be an elf. But, fuck me, he's a singer. What he was singing, though, was not rock'n'roll. It sounded more like...prog-folk. Like Jethro Tull's Living in the Past. Only a little bit proggier. And a little more folky. At one point, he even pulled out a wooden recorder and began playing it in a way that would have brought Mrs. Patterson, my old teacher, to tears. Finally, he switched out the recorder for something that looked like a cross between a bong and a rocket launcher. It was supposedly a bassoon.

We drank our beers and went backstage after Fang finished.
'Do you know who that singer is?' I inquired of a young man dressed in an out-of-date Fraternity T-shirt.
There was no denying that Bon Scott was no ordinary vocalist.

I'd want to tell you that I made a mental point to seek up all of Bon's past work, but Fang weren't really my cup of tea - and by the end of the night, we were fatigued and frazzled from the show and all the driving earlier in the day. So, teeth chattering in the cold, we returned to the B&B and decided to crack open the coin box on the meter so we could keep putting in the same 5p again and over.
It worked flawlessly. But just as we were getting warmed up...

Tap-tap-tap.
'What's that noise?' Tom wondered.
Tap-tap-tap.
'Shit!' hissed Vic. 'The landlady must have heard us breaking the currency box!' 'Quick, put it back on!'

A mad dash ensued as we attempted to unbreak the electric meter, until we noticed the knocking wasn't coming from the door. It was coming from the window.
Then we heard the whispers. 'Pssst. Hey? What's up, lads? Open the window! It's us... Fang!'

I was intoxicated and don't remember much, but when we pulled back the curtains, there was Bon and a couple of the boys from Fang shivering on the street outside. Their tour bus had broken down, which meant no heater - and because the bus's side panels were constructed of stainless steel, it had gotten as cold as a fridge inside. A mechanic was already working on it, they said, though I had no clue where they'd located a guy in Torquay at 11.30 p.m. on an Easter Monday who knew his way around a big-block American diesel. Whatever the case, Fang really needed to get out of the cold, especially since it had started to sleet again. So we pushed open the window sash and hauled the boys from Fang inside, trying not to wake the landlady. I'm not sure if this actually happened, but I was told it did. But, because I'm so inebriated, I have an excuse.

Fang's roadie eventually knocked on the window to say that he'd finally gotten the bus started again.
The following night, we performed in Plymouth Guildhall, once again with Fang in support.

I remember nothing about the show except that around two-thirds of the way through, I collapsed on stage and began to roll around, groaning and howling. The audience thought it was all part of the act and were going crazy, so I pulled myself back on my feet and continued with the song I was doing, but that was it - we finished twenty minutes early and I was off to A&E.

I'd gotten appendicitis. Fortunately, it was not severe enough to necessitate emergency surgery, but I did require a lengthy course of antibiotics.

The tour continued, night after night, six or seven days a week. We were travelling hundreds of kilometers per day, sometimes in the Granada, sometimes in the van. But we were so young and so eager - and our dreams were still so high - that it was a fantastic time.

I'm sorry to say I never saw Bon again. But it's strange to me that our destiny became intertwined on that cold night on the Torquay seafront.

I wish I could have gotten to know him better.

One of the most enjoyable aspects of creating the album for me was meeting André Jacquemin, a composer, producer, and arranger who had recently relocated his studio from his father's greenhouse to Red Bus's Wardour Street location. He was the person who produced all of Monty Python's albums - he'd later write the James Bond-esque theme song for Life of Brian - and being a huge Python fan myself, I couldn't get enough of his stories. André, on the other hand, nearly killed us both since he drove a Bond Bug, a three-wheeled 'microcar' fashioned like a wedge with screens instead of doors. It looked like a slice of orange with a sense of humour - it only came in that color - but André was so proud of it that he insisted on taking me for a ride, and we almost ended up under the wheels of a London bus.

Another unforgettable experience from those studio sessions was when we recorded our cover of 'The House of the Rising Sun,' which I'd first performed all those years earlier at Sunniside Working Men's Club. I thought I'd nailed the vocals after a few runs through it, but Roberto kept saying, 'It's just-a missing... something.' Then inspiration hit, and he began dashing around the studio, setting up microphones all over the place and making all these humming noises into them. When he was finished, the tune began with what sounded like a drone, which complemented the dramatic, foreboding tone of the song wonderfully.

Of course, no one ever heard it because no one bought the record.

We saw a trip of Australia and Japan as the solution to our difficulties, so we packed our bags and left in early 1974. Obviously, we had to seat in the back of the plane, but we stocked up on duty-free tabs and whisky and spent the most of the flight getting through it all.

Our first performance was a festival-style event at E. S. Marks Athletic Field, a large open-air arena with a covered grandstand, where we were the headliners. When we took the stage, it seemed like Woodstock - large stage, big sound system, huge throng of thousands of Australians, everyone yelling and whooping. It was amazing, and it was a huge morale lift.

But two days later, in the heat of the afternoon, when it was around 120 degrees in the shade, we were playing a working men's club out in the sticks. The place was a shambles. There are only tin cottages and rusted-out autos. The crowd was small, hot, and inebriated - and they didn't like Poms. Later, when we were removing our stage gear in the dressing room, a giant snake came, and the four of us raced screaming out of there in our underwear. We were Geordies, after all, and the only snakes we'd ever seen were in Tarzan movies. When we notified the venue manager, he mumbled 'Fucking Poms,' walked into the dressing room, emerged with the snake, and said, 'It's not even poisonous, you wankers.' At that moment, we began to think that it had been placed there on purpose.

By the time we arrived back in Sydney, we were beginning to wonder if the tour had ever been a smart idea in the first place. Meanwhile, we discovered these great parks where you could bring your own steak and beer and cook your own barbecue, and we went to watch The Exorcist, which terrified the living shit out of us.

The journey culminated in two nights at Chequers, Sydney's famous nightclub, and if I'd known where to look, I could have spotted Malcolm Young standing at the back on one of those nights. He'd gone there to collect up a check due to him by the venue management, but stayed for the event after hearing about my James Brown antics from Bon. I'm not sure whether it's true, but I heard Angus was there a week later when we played the Hornsby Police

Boys Club in Sydney's outskirts (not to see us, he was just there). Of course, there was no writhing on the floor and groaning for me on either of those nights - though, as usual, Tom Hill spent a good portion of both shows on my shoulders.

Then it was time to fly to Tokyo, where we were greeted by Mr. Udo, the famed promoter who had booked Led Zeppelin's tour of Japan a few years before.

If I recall correctly, we did four gigs in Japan, traveling between them by bullet train - something I'd heard about but nearly didn't believe existed. It was an incredible sensation to sit in the restaurant car of a train traveling at nearly 100 mph with no rattles or shaking. The Japanese were truly light-years ahead of everyone else.

The gigs, on the other hand, were weird occurrences. You'd perform a song and get a small round of polite applause at the conclusion, followed by quiet. You have to question if they even liked the music. Then, at one performance, a child became so enthralled that he stood up and applauded.
Security quickly apprehended him and threw him out.

We finished the year by supporting Deep Purple on their German tour. This was going to be exciting; they were incredibly massive. But the contrast between our triumph and Ritchie Blackmore's juggernaut was stark: despite a major line-up change that saw David Coverdale replace Ian Gillan on vocals, the current Deep Purple album Burn had become a Top 10 hit on both sides of the Atlantic.

I mean, the fans who came to such performances were only interested in one band. So, despite the fact that we were doing great and the band was tight, no one was paying attention.

Geordie needed to attempt something new after Don't Be Fooled by the Name failed to deliver a single hit. But what happened made no sense to me at all.

Vic simply vanished. I still have no idea what happened because no one told me. Vic had been our main lyricist and guitarist for a while.

He was out of the band the next thing you knew. Which seemed particularly unjust given that he was the one who had put the band together in the first place.

Micky Bennison, an old friend of Tom's, ended up being the lead guitarist. He was a charming kid with a fine guitar who loved American cars and ran an import company called Third Leg Motors. But by the time we'd written some new songs and on the road again... nobody cared. And when we played the old Geordie tunes without Vic's guitar sounds, they sounded so bleak and uninteresting. Worst of all, being locked in the back of a van with a guy I barely knew wasn't pleasant anymore. The team spirit had vanished.

Tom and the other Brian had clearly lost their excitement as well. When we returned from Germany, they opened a business in Newcastle called Geordie the Boutique, directly across the street from the Theatre Royal, and it took up the majority of their time. Tom was a bit of a fashionista, and he'd go shopping in London and bring back all the latest wares - the stuff you couldn't find up north - which they'd resale. They appeared lot more enthusiastic about it than Geordie.

Then, one night, a representative from EMI Records came up to Newcastle and took me out to dinner. He inquired as to what I was up to these days. 'To be honest, nothing much,' I said. Then he asked if I'd ever thought about working for a record label. 'Oh, I'd love to work for a record label,' I said, 'they always seem to have more money than me...'

'You might be a rep,' he said, looking me dead in the eye, and I understood this wasn't a hypothetical talk. He was truly interviewing me for a job.
'Do you honestly believe... I could do that?' I inquired.
'Of sure,' he replied. 'You're a funny man who gets along well with others and has appeared on Top of the Pops. That is exactly what we require. You'd be a tremendous asset to the firm.'
'Oh, mate,' I murmured, trying not to cry, 'that would be a dream come true—'
'We could also arrange for you to have a business automobile.'

'All right, where do I sign?' I said. I wasn't kidding.

Unfortunately for me, the EMI representative went out to dinner the next night with radio broadcaster James Whale, who was then a friend of mine and the host of Night Owls on Metro Radio. And, believing he was acting in my best interests, James persuaded the person out of making the deal official. 'Oh, no, no, Brian's no good for that, he's a singer!' he exclaimed. 'You can't wreck his career by giving him a record contract!'

I had the option of killing him. I mean, I really needed the money. 'Why did you say that, you fucking moron?!' James made no apologies. He said he'd merely spoken his thoughts, that he honestly believed I was meant for greater things. I couldn't decide whether to thank you or fuck you.

At home, things were bad. But I couldn't bear the thought of going back to Parsons, cap in hand, and asking for my old position. The arrogant 'I told you so' lectures from people like Harry Blair would be insufferable. Besides, my prior employment probably didn't exist in the first place. As for going on the dole, I was too proud to accept government assistance.

8. Stowaway

The mansion was in Preston Grange, an affluent neighbourhood near Tyne-mouth Golf Club. I could never have afforded something like it on my own. It was brand new, with large modern windows, central heating, a garage, a driveway, and a back yard - the ideal home for a young middle-class family. It felt too amazing to be true, given how few records Geordie had sold since our one and only Top 10 single.

I reminded myself that Ellis was receiving a new record in exchange. And it wasn't unheard of for a band like ours to make a mid-career comeback back then, even if Vic, the driving force behind it all, was no longer with us.

It was going to be a difficult balancing act, though. On the one hand, we needed to move on from the old Geordie and stop drawing similarities to Slade. On the other hand, we didn't want to lose our former supporters... or the few of them we still had.

Red Bus was at least taking the project seriously, as seen by the hiring of Philip 'Pip' Williams as producer - he'd previously worked with The Kinks and The Moody Blues and would go on to produce Status Quo's Rockin' All Over the World. So we were in good hands. But, of course, Red Bus, always trying to save money, had only allowed us a few days of studio time. And because production on the songs had begun before Vic was sacked, the material was all over the place.

The lead single was 'She's a Teaser,' a tight, hard-rocking piece that had a lot of brass added in the studio, making it sound like a bit of a sell-out. (That song had been completed long before the main album sessions began.)

All of the supporting tracks had already been completed by the time I arrived in London to record the vocals. That should have been a red flag. I mean, there was no band spirit at all. When Pip played the tapes back for me, I couldn't hide my dismay.

'I know what you're thinking,' Pip remarked. 'They're not quite there yet. That's why you're here...'

The next several days were the closest I'd ever come to working with a producer - and it taught me a lot of respect for what it takes to accomplish that job. To be a competent producer, you have to be a United Nations-worthy diplomat, a musical genius, and a technological wizard all rolled into one. Pip was all of those things and more. He also looked the part, wearing this magnificent buckskin jacket with all the tassels on the arms, much like an American frontiersman would have. It was the coolest, most rock'n'roll outfit I'd ever seen.

So there I was, with the words and a basic notion of the tune, just trying to make it work. And, of course, the first few times I went through it, I was just trying to get to the end without messing it up - that's always the way, unless you wrote the song yourself - but after that, I started to loosen up, improvise a little, and have some fun.

Pip has the amazing ability to gauge my emotions and respond accordingly. 'Let's take a break, Brian, we've worked long enough,' he'd say. Do you think you could handle another hour after dinner? I don't like vocalists who perform after dinner.'
Of all, I was still a young man at the time, so I reasoned that I could sing after anything.

The worst portions were mealtimes because I couldn't afford to eat out. Pip would identify a restaurant he wanted to go to, then look at me and say, 'Oh... is it pricey there?' To circumvent the problem, I ended up packing sandwiches. I mean, eating out wasn't something I was used to. Even at the height of Geordie's fame - when we were on Top of the Pops every other week - a meal out for us meant stopping at a Little Chef roadside café on the A1 or the inevitable Indian restaurant.

Even the best Michelin-starred cuisine couldn't compete with a Little Chef 'Olympic breakfast' when you were ravenous at 6 a.m. after a night of driving.

After we finished approximately a dozen tracks in three days, Pip took me out for a drink to celebrate.

'I'd love to, Pip,' I replied, 'but my train home leaves at 7 p.m. - so I'd best get going.'

'Well, you're getting close,' he replied as he checked his watch. 'Come on, let's hail a black cab.'

'I'll take the Tube, Pip, that's fine.'

'You'll never be on time taking the Tube, Brian. They're already on strike. You require a taxi.'

That's when I realized I just had enough money for the Underground fare, a beer, and a lunch on the way home. Pip told me not to say anything else. Then he reached into his pocket and brought out a £20 note, which is roughly £150 today. I told him I couldn't possibly accept that much money. However, he stuffed it inside my jeans pocket. 'Please, Brian,' he pleaded, 'I want you to accept it.'

We were standing outside, waiting for a cab a few minutes later. Pip pointed to my faded denim jacket, which had to be from The Gobi Desert Kanoe Klub days. It was ancient and in disrepair. 'How long have you had it?' he inquired.

'I'm not sure,' I said, shrugging. 'Why?'

'Try this on,' he added, taking off his own beautiful buckskin jacket. 'You'll look fantastic in it.'

'Pip, I can't take your jacket off,' I argued, 'I've only known you for three days!' And, by the way, where did you obtain that thing? It had to cost an arm and a leg!'

'Three days in a studio, Brian, is a long time. We've become buddies. And the jacket looks better on you.'

'Pip, I just can't, I'm fine - stop giving me stuff!'

Then a cab arrived, and Pip went away, leaving the jacket on the floor in front of me. 'I'll see you later, Brian,' he said over his shoulder. 'We wish you safe travels home. Take the jacket, too! You're a rock star, so dress accordingly.'

That was a memorable occasion for me. When I took it up and put it on, I felt like I was stealing it. It also made everything else I was wearing look filthy and worn-out, especially my shoes.

'King's Cross station,' I said through the window to the driver. He nodded, and I climbed into the back... praying to God that my brother Maurice was on the train.

If you're wondering why Maurice doesn't appear more frequently in this book, it's because he was away for the majority of the time.
He decided to be a chef at the age of fifteen, when I was just starting full-time at Parsons, and went to work at The County Hotel, opposite Newcastle's Central Station. First, they forced him work as a bellboy. He then advanced to become a commis waiter, or apprentice waiter, and then a commis chef. He'd practice at home as well. 'Boiled potatoes, Ma'am?' he'd ask my mother as he served Sunday supper. 'Would you like some carrots, Ma'am?'

Then one night, we discovered him packing his belongings. He told us he was heading to Jersey, in the Channel Islands, to work at a much larger hotel in St. Helier, the main town. Because Maurice didn't say much, it was the first time any of us had heard of it. There were no heartfelt goodbyes. He simply boarded the train and left.

The next thing we knew, he'd returned with a Mod-style Lambretta scooter, complete with twin chrome tail pipes and a spare tyre on the rear. It was fantastic. Although the spare wheel was stolen the first time I borrowed it to go to the movies. Which I still regret to this day.

Then Maurice took off again, this time with a Triumph Spitfire sports vehicle.
When I got home and saw it parked outside our house, I thought to myself, 'Whose is that?' Nothing like that existed on our estate. Maurice then emerged, but I didn't recognize him because he'd grown another foot and a moustache.

He made me take off all my dirty work clothes and wash my hands before taking me for a trip in the car - he had the leather gloves, the herringbone cloth cap, the complete old-school driving get-up. Twice. I didn't hold it against him. What a magnificent machine the Spitfire was. It had all of the knobs, gauges, and buttons, as well as indicator stalks, and when you changed gears, the engine produced all of these satanic woofling noises.

Maurice had me in amazement. I'd always been an excellent student in school - until the end, anyway - and I worked at one of the world's greatest engineering firms while also doing side jobs. But I was bankrupt. Meanwhile, Maurice, who had failed every test he'd ever taken, was driving around in this.

But here's the thing about Maurice. He acts stupid, although he's smarter than everyone. And he's the most endearing person you'll ever meet. People have been approaching me and asking, 'How's Maurice?' for as long as I can remember. 'I adore Maurice.' He's just another one of those guys.

Anyway... after returning from Jersey for real, Maurice acquired a job as chief steward on the London to Newcastle train service, in the first-class section. And if you happened to be on the same train as him, even in the cheapest seat available, he would unfailingly look after you. In those days, everyone cared after each other's families. It was an unspoken norm. But Maurice, being a nice young man, offered the courtesy to his pals as well. Brendan Healy, a close friend who frequently had to travel to London for auditions - more on Brendan and his many talents later - was dubbed 'The Good Samaritan of King's Cross'.

I heard Maurice's voice before I saw him.
'Brian???'
Instant relief. Then I looked around and saw him hanging out of the first-class carriage.
'Are you going to a Cowboys and Indians fancy dress party?' he inquired, glancing at my jacket.
'Fuck off, Maurice,' I said, smiling.
'Come on, get yourself in here.'

It was a well-oiled routine with Maurice. You'd stroll methodically past the restaurant car, ticket in hand, as if heading to your seat in economy class, then a service door would open next to you, and you'd sneak inside. Then you'd sit against the wall in the kitchen, out of sight, smoking a cigarette until the train started moving. A wink and a nod would be exchanged before you were taken to a window seat in the dining carriage, with a white tablecloth in front of you, and proceeded to enjoy a silver-service steak dinner with as many beers as you could drink.

'Boiled potatoes, sir?' Maurice would ask with a flourish to ensure that none of the paying passengers were aware of what was going on. 'And would you like some carrots, sir?'

The nicest part of the voyage, of course, was when the train crossed the River Tyne to Central Station, those last few seconds providing the most amazing view of the Tyne Bridge, all lit up from beneath. That was the lovely thing about the King's Cross to Newcastle rail service: it made coming home seem so pleasant.

The album vanished without a trace. There were no survivors. Not even a life belt was discovered. But, unlike the Mary Celeste, there was no mystery here - the album was plain bad.

To be sure, the marketing had been abysmal.
Red Bus' response to the challenge of Geordie needing to move on without alienating our previous fans was to create it a 'faceless' album with a cover picturing a naked woman shooting out of the earth holding up a dazzling light. The title was Save the World, starring Brian Johnson. But, of course, the record did not save anything. Not the whole globe. Certainly not Geordie.

I recall Maurice driving over to the Preston Grange house one morning and saying, "So, what's up with the record?" I've heard nothing on the radio...'
I told him it hadn't been officially released yet - which it hadn't - but an album is normally heavily promoted well before it's published. But neither of the two songs we'd released - 'She's a Teaser' and 'Goodbye Love' - had even gone close to chart success.

'Can I at least hear it?' Maurice said.
'I don't have a copy,' I shrugged, and that was true. I mean, it was difficult to care when no one else did...

People frequently ask me how and when Geordie and I split up. But, in reality, we never did. There was no significant fight or walkout. We didn't lose anyone to alcohol or drugs. Our record label never even dropped us.

It all kind of... faded away.

9. A Message from Above

After my training was completed, I was given my own Transit van with an orange light on top, and I was told that I would be on-call every other two nights. I also got my own walkie-talkie and, even better, my own call sign - 'Whisky Oscar, One-One-One'. I'll admit you that it wasn't the coolest of call signals - and good luck pronouncing it after a few beers - but I couldn't have cared less because I was in love with my new job.

It wasn't only that I was finally free of Red Bus and all the nonsense of the music industry. And it wasn't simply that I was finally making a livelihood. When I was out in my small vehicle... I felt like I was doing something meaningful.

You have to remember that back then, if your windscreen broke while driving down the A1, you couldn't just pick up the phone and ask for help. You had to get out of the car and walk to the nearest emergency phone. And if you were a long way between phones, or if it was dark and pissing it down - and as I may have already indicated, it was frequently pissing it down - it could be a terrifying, grueling experience. If you're not careful, you could wind yourself freezing to death in the winter. In 1970s Britain, the first phone you tried didn't always work. That meant you had to walk to the next one. Then all the way back to your car.

Needless to say, most people were overjoyed to see me by the time my van arrived - and it gave me great pleasure to see a family of four in their little Austin Maxi toddle off when I got them back on the road. I even considered starting my own business because I'd embraced the idea that this was going to be my life from now on. I hadn't given up singing; I'd just convinced myself to approach it as a pastime now. Even if a part of me yearned to prove that I could do more and compete with the best of them.

Of course, there were days when fixing windscreens was a chore. For starters, it was strenuous physical labor, and you'd come home with glass and adhesive in your hair and sticky, black hands from handling the windscreen rubber. And consumers might be challenging - or simply bizarre - at times.

One night, about 11.30 p.m., I was called to a large articulated lorry with its front window broken. This was in Scotch Corner, about fifty miles south of Newcastle. And, of course, it was raining at the time, and there was a fierce storm blowing.

Now, the glass for a lorry is enormous and quite heavy, and the only way I could reach the opening was to stand on the roof of the van. I was afraid the wind would get me - or the glass - so I asked the driver, 'Is there any chance you could hold one end while I get it into place?' He looked back at me, unscrewed the cap of his flask, poured himself a good hot cup of tea, and went, 'Not my job'.

That was a fantastic night.
Then there was the day I was called to a Ford Cortina in the middle of nowhere, only to find the driver sitting in the boot, drinking from a mound of small whisky bottles, completely out of his mind. On closer inspection, both the front and rear windscreens were missing.

When I saw that mess, it gave me the creeps.
Whatever he'd hit had gone in one end so fast that it came out the other. I'd never seen anything like it before. And he had all the booze in the boot because he was a whisky salesman from Edinburgh who was dropping off samples at all the hotels along the A1.

He was completely incomprehensible.
'B... br...' he couldn't get the words out. 'Fucking, Bri...' I assumed he said bird. It had to be a monster.
'No, brick...' he finally managed. That explains why it had gone straight through. It's no surprise he was paralyzed. The brick had become wedged between the two back tyres of a truck he was following, clawed its way free, and then blasted right through his car, missing his head by inches.

Then I gazed back at him, wondering how he'd ever get himself in shape enough to drive the hundred-odd miles back home. But those were different times. People did crap every day of their lives that you'd be locked up for today. But I'd done my best for him. And he did leave me six bottles of whisky as a tip.

I honestly don't think there was a faster, harder-working windscreen fitter in the entire country by the time Margaret Thatcher became Britain's new prime leader in May 1979. That was my specialty. And I was making money. In fact, if it hadn't been for what happened next, I might never have given it up...

My walkie-talkie went off at three or four o'clock in the afternoon, just as rush hour was starting. 'Brian?' asked the dispatcher. 'Please hurry, son, we've got a black Ford Cortina Mark IV just north of Scotch Corner. They're in a hurry.'

A brand-new Cortina Mark IV was a very lovely ride back then, and it would look great in black. So, when I stepped into the van and headed off towards the A1, I knew I was in for a treat.

I was not mistaken.

I could tell this job would be different from the moment I laid eyes on it. There were two men at the rear, one of them was wearing a panama hat and black glasses. Another two guys, all dressed in black, were outside, smoking and leaning on the bonnet. They just had this sense of... freedom about them. They felt as if they didn't belong in the usual, nine-to-five environment. It was something I hadn't seen in a long time. Something I really missed...

'What's your name?' said one of the smokers, his voice silky and powerful.
'Brian,' I said.
'OK, Brian,' he said. 'Let me explain the situation. We've got a VIP in the back, and he'll be on stage at the Hammersmith Odeon at 9 p.m. tonight. It's 4.15 p.m. now, and it's a five-hour drive to London... maybe a little less if we put our foot down.' He pointed to the damaged windscreen of the Cortina. 'How quickly can you get a fresh one of these in? There are 3,500 people counting on us to arrive at the location on time.'
Holy sh*t, I thought.
'Give me fifteen minutes,' I said.
'C'mon, son. Realistically... how long?'
'Fifteen minutes.'

I worked so quickly it felt like I was in a trance. I easily removed the old windscreen in under two minutes. Then I dove inside the cabin with the portable vacuum, avoiding the impulse to spy on the V.I.P. in the back. Then I dashed back to the van. I found the replacement glass. The new rubber was applied. Then I looped the cable around the channel, brought the glass over to the car, and bash-yanked it over the opening - bash-yank, bash-yank, bash-yank - until it finally locked into place over the lip.
'Done,' I murmured, sweat streaming down my cheeks.
'That wasn't fifteen minutes,' the person said. 'It was more like twelve. 'How bad is it?'
'Twenty-five pounds.'
He took out his wallet, took out two crisp twenty, and shoved them into my hand.
'Keep the change,' he said.

Oh my god.
Then he stepped into the driver's seat, started the engine, and started pulling away... just as I realized I hadn't asked the V.I.P.'s name.
But I knew because the automobile pulled to a halt as the back window drew up alongside me. The glass fell to the ground. Then a pale, hairy arm appeared, holding up a T-shirt.

'Here you go,' a voice whispered in a Cockney accent that made me shiver.
The voice was distinct. It was being played all over the radio at the time, at all hours of the day, all over the world. It was impossible for me to believe. Ian Dury, whose recent hit, 'Hit Me with Your Rhythm Stick,' was currently at No. 1 in the UK charts, was personally handing me a T-shirt.

I took the T-shirt, dumbfounded, while starring at myself in Dury's spectacles.
The window rolled up again...
The Cortina then sped away, wheels squealing, in the direction of Hammersmith Odeon.
I wished it were me, I thought.

While attempting to regain my breath, I looked down at the black T-shirt with the words 'IAN DURY AND THE BLOCKHEADS' written in white on it. My entire nervous system felt like it was on fire. Not only had I met a rock'n'roll legend. I suddenly knew I could do it again, even though I was in my forties and had already tried and failed once.

Of course, the truth was that it wasn't even an option.
I belonged around that energy, that sensation of freedom.
It wasn't only a part of who I was.
It was my fault.
I needed to find a way back into the game.

Part Three
10. Beautiful Mover

The phone in the vinyl business never stopped ringing in the early weeks of 1980. A dealership with six new autos to sell. A new club booking. An audition invitation. My mother has invited me to bring the kids home for Sunday lunch. Another club booking. On the phone with Ellis' Soho office. I was so exhausted.

Then, one early March morning, I took up the phone and heard a woman on the other end of the line with a heavy East German accent. And, perhaps because I'd seen too many war movies, she sounded like she was prepared to give me the third degree.

'Is that Brian Yonson?' she inquired.
'Who's asking?' I answered.
'Zat is unimportant. What is vital is that you come to Londe-on to sink wiss a gruppe.'
'Sink?'
'Sink. 'You're Brian Yonson, ze sinker, ja?'
'Oh, you mean singer... well, that's me. And, uh... what exactly do you want me to do again?'
'Sink.'
'Yes, I got that part...'
'Wit eine rockgruppe.'
'OK, look, I'm sorry, but I've stopped doing auditions. I'm already in a band, and we're about to—'
'I can't tell you the name of zis gruppe.'
'Okay, well, that's probably just as well, because, as I previously stated, I'm not doing any more auditions.'
There was a long delay. 'If you knew my name, you wouldn't be saying nein,' she said.
I was becoming irritated at this point since I needed to get back to work... but I was also interested. 'Look, if this "rock gruppen" is that big a deal,' I said,'maybe you can give me a hint?'
Another extended pause. Then a long sigh. 'I suppose I can tell you ze initials,' she said.
'All right, then...'

'A. Z.'

I racked my thoughts, but no band came to mind. 'I'm sorry,' I responded, 'but that doesn't really ring a bell—'Und D. Z.'

It was now my time to be very silent. Because I was having problems believing my own ears. I mean, there was no way this woman worked for...

'You mean... AC/DC?!'

'Scheisse! I've said far too much!'

Before I go any further, I should probably note that the time between the show at Lobley Hill and the call from the East German woman had been quite frustrating.

That was mostly due to Davy Whittaker's supervisor, who had buried his claws in and refused to give him any time off during the week so we could go to London and start laying down some tracks. Red Bus had their own studio by this point, and that's where they wanted us to record - but there wasn't enough time between Davy clocking off on a Friday evening and him clocking back in on a Monday morning to drive the 300 miles down there and back and get any real work done in between. We did get one song recorded - 'Rockin' with the Boys,' written by yours truly with Derek and Dave Robson - but Red Bus wouldn't release it until a complete album's worth of material was ready. But, until we had a hit record, Davy was never going to leave his job - and, in the meantime, his boss was never going to allow him a day off to help him with his musical career. It was a classic Catch-22 situation.

I eventually took matters into my own hands and called Davy's supervisor myself - maybe not the best choice. Davy worked as a delivery driver for Calor Gas, and he knew all of the company's clients, where they lived, and what kind of gas they required and when, so his boss didn't want to lose him.

I understood I didn't have a leg to stand on the moment the guy answered the phone. It wasn't like I was famous or anything. All I could do was appeal to his sense of fairness.

'Hello, my name is Brian,' I introduced myself. 'I'm Davy's band's singer. We've been offered the opportunity to record in London. Davy will be back by Thursday if we travel down to London on a Sunday night and stay in a hotel.'
'No,' was the response.
'... may I inquire as to why?' I inquired.
'No.'
'Have you even considered this, or are you just saying "no" because you can?'
'Yesterday, the answer was no. Today, the answer is no. And the answer tomorrow will be no.'
'Oh, come on, give the youngster a chance!' I blurted out. 'He's a fantastic drummer, and this is a fantastic opportunity for us. Surely you have someone who can fill in for him? He'll be back in four days and can work additional shifts to make up for it.'
'I'll fire him if he travels to London,' he replied.
That was a little much for me. 'You know what I mean?' I asked.
'You're a fucking arsehole,' he says.
'Pardon me?'
'YOU... ARE A FUCKING... ARSEHOLE,' he says.
Slam.

Davy eventually worked at Calor Gas until he retired, which made no sense to me.
To say I was conflicted when I got a call from AC/DC would be an understatement. I mean, the moment I heard the band's name, I was reminded of the horrible tragedy from just a few weeks before.

Ken had been the one to break the news to me at the record store.
'Hey Brian, you know that song "Whole Lotta Rosie" you sing?'
'Yeah?'
'The individual who sings it is no longer alive.'
'No, he isn't. He was just on Top of the Pops. He's as in shape as a butcher's dog.'
'Well, it states here that he was discovered dead inside someone's automobile - "death by misadventure" they call it.'
'What? That can't be right... hand it over.'

I took the paper from him and read the tale for myself... but I couldn't figure out what had happened. I was absolutely unaware of the consequences of binge drinking or using illegal drugs back then. Part of it was because no one in my environment had enough money for drugs, and we all had to get up at the crack of dawn most days to go to work, so being drunk to the point of passing out wasn't an option. Meanwhile, I'd never smoked a joint, and as for harsher drugs, I'd never been offered them, and I'd never met someone who'd used them; they were utterly out of my league. So it astounded me that a young man like Bon, who was just a year older than me, fighting fit, and in the prime of his life, could die in such a manner.

Most of all, the tragedy struck me - not only for Bon's family, bandmates, and friends, but for anybody who loved rock music. 'Whole Lotta Rosie,' in my opinion, was one of the greatest rock songs of all time, and it was just one of many classics he'd written and recorded with AC/DC, from Let There Be Rock to Dirty Deeds Done Dirt Cheap. And, of course, Bon and the boys had excelled themselves with their Highway to Hell album the previous summer. They'd finally broken through to become a major headline act after six years of nonstop gigging thanks to that gem - and the title song about the hardships of life on the road.

Meanwhile, the album had reached No. 8 in the British charts and No. 17 in America, where they were becoming even more popular than in Europe. With their second single, 'Touch Too Much,' the lads even made it to the top of the charts. I'd seen it myself at home only a few weeks before. Bon appeared to be having the time of his life. After all, he had to have known that AC/DC were on their way to becoming a massive band thanks to Highway to Hell.

Meanwhile, it hadn't occurred to me that Bon was the guy from Fang with whom I'd shivered in frigid Torquay seven years before. And it would take some time...

The East German woman who'd called me wouldn't tell me her name, so I came up with one myself - 'Olga from the Volga'. Olga, from what I could see, worked at the office of Peter Mensch, a tour accountant turned manager, but everytime I asked her a question, she responded with either stony silence or 'Zis, I cannot answer.'

What perplexed me was how my name landed up on their list of performers to contact. It didn't make any sense. It had been seven years since Geordie's string of minor hit singles, and I was only a household name in the sense that everyone in my house knew what I was talking about.

What I'd discover later - much later - was that my name had been submitted by numerous different persons. There was an AC/DC fan in Cleveland, Ohio, who'd seen Geordie back in the day and recommended to Peter Mensch that the band try me out. Then there was Robert 'Mutt' Lange, the young South African producer of Highway to Hell, who knew Geordie and had also introduced me to Angus and Malcolm. And I later discovered that Bon had also told them about me following our Torquay encounter.

The other question on my mind was whether Angus, Malcolm, and the other lads would want to go on without Bon. Again, it would be a while before I got the complete tale, but if it hadn't been for Bon's parents, Isa and Chick (Chick was short for Charles), the answer might have been 'no' - at least not right then. They told Angus and Malcolm that Bon would have wanted AC/DC to continue working on the album they'd recently begun. At the very least, they hoped it would provide a welcome distraction for the band, providing some solace and assisting them in dealing with their sadness.

My thoughts was racing by the time I hung up the phone with Olga.
Of course, I was thrilled and excited to get the call. It almost didn't feel real, auditioning for a band known all over the world. But I also knew there would be scores of other applicants vying for the same job, and I wasn't sure I had the heart to go through all the anticipation and disappointment, especially when my small band was doing so well.

Brian, please gather yourself. Set the record straight. You're 32 years old and live with your mum and father. You have a thriving small business and a successful small band. You're content with your girlfriend, you have two wonderful girls, you can afford stuff for them - everything is fine. Why would you do something like this? I'll tell you why - I have no choice.

But first, how am I going to get to London on such short notice?
My vinyl jobs for that day would have to be canceled. Meanwhile, Ken required the Austin Maxi for work - the week of the intended audition was particularly busy - and my own car at the time was a wildly unstable Jaguar XJ with a mind of its own and a foul temper.

'I guess I'm going to have to say no,' I said Ken after explaining the nature of the call.
'Oh, you've got to try that, Brian,' he added.
'Look, I'm not going to get it in the first place,' I said, already beginning to talk myself out of it. 'They'll hire someone they know, most likely another Aussie.'
'Why don't you sleep on it,' Ken advised.

Before I could call Olga from the Volga back with my response, another call came in from nowhere.
It was my old friend André Jacquemin this time. We stayed in touch, and he went on to establish Redwood Studios in London.

'Would you like to earn £350?' he inquired.
'Look, André, anything you want me to do for that kind of money,' I answered, 'the answer's yes.'
'Great,' he exclaimed. 'All you have to do is come to London for a day and record a jingle for a Hoover commercial. Now, I can't guarantee they'll use your take - you're competing with a very huge lady who sings gospel music - but you'll get paid regardless.'
Even before he finished his sentence, the gears in my head began to turn.
'... and, uh, when do you need me to be there?' I inquired.
He chose the date, which coincided with the intended AC/DC audition.
'Let me speak with my business partner,' I grinned. It wasn't simply the AC/DC gig that made me happy. I'd also never done any commercial work before, and I was excited about the prospect of

completing a session at a brand-new, cutting-edge facility like Redwood.

Ken came in and saw my expression.
'What makes you so happy?' he inquired.
I told him about the phone call.
'Brian, I think someone up there is trying to tell you something,' he grinned.

After considering how to go to London, I decided to throw caution to the wind and take the Jag. Then I drove down the A1 to meet André at Redwood Studios.
I felt fucking wonderful after singing about a vacuum cleaner's sucking power. My contract even contained repetition fees, which were unheard of in the 1970s rock'n'roll industry.

Finally, at 3.30 p.m., it was time to drive the three miles southwest across London to Pimlico - the journey took only about fifteen minutes back then - where I'd been told there was a rehearsal room and recording facility called Vanilla Studios in the back of a commercial garage. That's where I'd meet the band for my audition.

I'd been up since the crack of dawn and driven 300 miles by the time I arrived and found a parking spot, and there was still some time to kill before my 5 p.m. audition. So I ducked into an ancient café, reminiscent of pre-war London. I requested a cup of tea and a beef pie. The woman at the desk had a cigarette dangling from her lips, ash flying everywhere when she spoke. It didn't bode good for hygiene. The fact that the pie crust would not budge with a toothpick, knife, or nail was a sign of its age and pedigree. So, in the name of health and safety, I got up from the table, put on my cap, and decided to face the unknown on the other side of the street instead.

It's a wonder I ever discovered the studio entrance, it was so tucked away.
But I did, and then I was inside, greeted by the AC/DC road crew, who were in the middle of a game of pool. I'd put a cent on the table, it was my turn to play, and we were having a wonderful old chat and laugh.

I'd imagined the band was busy with something and would come and get me, but instead they were in the rehearsal room, gazing at their watches, wondering where the fuck the guy from Newcastle was. The band's tour manager, Ian Jeffery, was eventually deployed as a search party.
'Has anyone seen that Geordie lad?'
'Well, I'm a Geordie,' I explained.
The crew glanced at me, shocked. 'Are you Brian?' I nodded. 'Oh, for fuck's sake, we've been waiting for you for an hour!'
Nobody had bothered to ask me because I looked like a working boy. If the lads were annoyed, they kept it to themselves. In fact, they couldn't have made me feel more at ease. 'I assume this is your local brew?' said Malcolm, handing out a bottle of Newcastle Brown Ale to me. It was so Malcolm of him.

'Oh, I could kill one of those,' I chuckled. 'Many thanks, mate.'
'What do you want to sing, mate?' Malcolm inquired casually.
Oh, Jesus. What a question. I didn't want to start with an AC/DC song because they'd know it by heart and I'd be fumbling around, which wouldn't be exactly an equal playing field. So I played Tina Turner's classic "Nutbush City Limits." Angus, who hadn't said anything, appeared surprised yet unconcerned.
'Well, you passed the first test,' Malcolm remarked flatly.
'So, what is it?' I inquired.
'You didn't say "Smoke on the Water". "Nutbush" is a good tune,' he adds. 'Is everyone ready?'
'What key?' Angus eventually questioned.
'Do you think it's A?' I answered.
Malcolm looked at me and replied, 'A? 'Are you sure?'
'Yeah.'

You see, A is the high rock'n'roll key - it's Robert Plant territory. The rock'n'roll key to all rock'n'roll keys.
Then Malcolm remarked, 'Hang on, I think I've got it.'
Then Phil and Cliff joined in, Angus arrived, heads began to rock, and off we went. They were waiting to hear this voice, to see if it was worth their time, and it was the most exhilarating moment of my life.

I mean, I was in a fine small band, but nothing prepared me for that sound. It was the best thing I'd ever felt or heard, and I began singing as if my life depended on it.

'That was a lot of fun,' I added afterwards, almost welling up, for it had truly been magical, at least for me.
But then came the true test.
'Can you try anything of ours now?' Malcolm inquired. 'Just name a song, any song...'
I didn't have to think about it.
'"Whole Lotta Rosie," I said.

No matter how amazing it felt to play 'Nutbush,' 'Whole Lotta Rosie' was nearly an out-of-body experience. As soon as we started, I started getting strange tingles and goosebumps. I had the impression that Bon was in the room with us, smiling and sipping his rum and Coke. Remember, he'd only been gone a month. And there I was, in that tiny room, performing his hallmark song, with Angus next to me, this amazing force of energy. The hairs on my arms stood on end when he tore into the solo. Every member of the band is performing as if their lives depended on it. It was the AC/DC way. It sounded perfect. This was rock'n'roll. This was the way it was supposed to be. Then it was over, and I was walking out of the room.

'Thanks, fellas,' I said, thinking that was the end of it. 'The boys back home would never believe I did this. I can't wait to tell them...'
A young man named Peter Mensch followed me out. He couldn't have been more than twenty-seven at the time, with his bushy brows, ruffled hair, and New York accent. He appeared to be a pretty cool, easygoing music manager.
'Hey, Brian, where are you going?' he inquired.
'Oh, I've had to drive back home,' I said. 'I've had three Ford Cortinas and a Datsun Cherry waiting for me in the shop, and they all needed vinyl roofing yesterday.'
'No, no, no,' Peter responded, 'the lads would want you to remain...'
'Ah, I wish I could,' I admitted. 'But I'm the only one who can fit the roofs, so I really need to get going.'

It was now about 8.30 p.m. I couldn't believe how swiftly time had passed.
'Well, at least come back inside and have one more of those Newcastle Browns before you leave.'
'Mate, it's a five-hour drive back up the A1, so I won't get home until 1.30 a.m. - and I have to open the shop at nine. Then I've got a gig tomorrow night...'

Peter threw up his hands and gave me a disapproving look.
'Can I at least give you a call when you return?' he inquired.
'Anytime,' I replied.
That'll be the last I hear from him, I reasoned.

11. Breaking Up

If there was ever a time in my life when I wanted to tell someone good news, this was it. However, there was no one to tell. Ken had long since left. My mother and father were still away. It was excruciating. I felt like I was going to burst. Except for the bottle of Famous Grouse I'd brought for my father's birthday, there wasn't a drop of alcohol in the house. And I couldn't even drink it. However... this was an emergency. And my grandfather would certainly understand. Oh, fuck it, I thought as I opened it and took a gulp. Then I just stood there, looking around the room, thinking, here I am, 32 years old, living with my parents in the same council house I grew up in, with the same view over the railway line to the power station and Vickers tank factory, and now I've just received a phone call that's going to change everything... maybe forever. The kind of phone call that most people never receive.

I took another swig... and another... and another...
My father arrived from his club. My mother was close following.
'Happy birthday, Dad,' I said as I raised the whisky. 'I've got something for you.'
My father gave me a strange look. 'Did you also eat my cake?'
'Oh, I'm sorry,' I said, realizing the bottle had been invaded. 'I'll get you another.'
'You're absolutely correct.'
'It's simply... I was offered a job, Dad. It's a big one. So I decided to celebrate.'
'A job?' he inquired. 'And with whom?'
'AC/DC.'

With a moan, my father sat in his chair. 'You say AC/DC? 'Didn't they just become nationalized?'
I buried my face in my hands. 'Dad, they're a rock band.'
'Oh, well... I've never heard of them.' In my father's opinion, if he hadn't heard of a band, it meant they hadn't achieved any kind of meaningful success. The Beatles, on the other hand, were a bit of a challenge for him.
My mother then entered.

'I got a new job, Ma,' I told her, overjoyed. 'I'm AC/DC's new lead singer!'
'Oh, son, that's a-nice,' she said. 'Do you want a sandwich?'

It was unthinkable. It had no meaning for them. In their opinion, becoming a professional musician with a band was the root of all my issues. So the prospect of me doing it again - and giving up my business - just reaffirmed their greatest suspicions that I was doomed.
At least Maurice got it. 'AC/DC?' he asked when I called. 'They're cunning, them.'
After the Grand National, which was won by Ben Nevis, the horse my father had backed, it was time for me to go to Westerhope Comrades Club for Geordie II's show that night.

The place had sold out, as usual, with a line out the door and halfway down the street. (I think I still have the flyer - entrance was 55p.) Dave Black's band Goldie was also on the bill that night. And because Dave Robson's brother Geoff was also in Goldie, it felt like a family affair.

I was sitting in the audience, listening to Goldie play their hit tune, 'Making Up Again,' when this girl approached me and said, 'I heard AC/DC hired a new singer, but you should have been ideal for it.' And I just smiled and nodded, as if I were in one of those movie scenarios where everything gets quiet around you because you know something big is about to happen but you can't say anything about it.

All I could think about was how I was going to get out of this life I'd created for myself. I'm going to crush my bandmates' hopes. My girlfriend's heart will be broken. I'm going to fire Ken, who is a kind guy. And there's always the danger that it'll all go wrong.

What I couldn't have realized was that the golden age of working men's clubs would be over in just a few years, and they'd all begin to close down. Meanwhile, the vinyl roof craze would go away as swiftly as it had begun. In other words, staying in Newcastle would have been a lot higher risk than joining AC/DC.

But that night at Westerhope Comrades Club, I felt like I'd buried a bomb that would kill everyone around me if it exploded. And all I could do was sit there, practicing what I was going to say, trying to figure out how to explain why being excited and sad at the same time makes you cry.

The day before I left for London to start my new work was about as bad as you'd expect.
My appointment hadn't been made public yet, but I needed to tell people closest to me.
The most difficult aspect was telling my girlfriend. She just knew she'd lost me. Not because I didn't want to be with her anymore, but because she wanted to settle down, which would be difficult if I was in a band. She was devastated. 'Please,' she said, 'I don't want to lose you.' It was truly heartbreaking. I mean, she was attractive and elegant; we might have had a lovely life together. But I'd given up on having a normal life when I left Parsons.

Then it was time to go inform Ken. 'Look, it's going to take a couple of months to record this album and see how it does, and if I don't come back, the business is yours,' I told him. He appeared pleased, but I was concerned that it would all fall apart after I left - after all, the main reason we were doing well was the quality of our work, but I was the one who did the majority of the fitting.

Finally, I had to organize a band meeting at the pub with the two Daves and Derek in Geordie II.
Of course, they were taken aback. 'Look, I've been offered this job, but it hasn't been announced yet, and I'm not sure what's going to happen, but it looks real, and I'm travelling to London tomorrow to start working on the new record,' I explained. I just need a little more time.'

The atmosphere was that of a funeral.
'Jesus, I thought we were going to make it,' Davy murmured, looking into his pint.
'So, Heaton Buffs is off?' Derek inquired.
'Everything's off... for now,' I muttered, and I could see the horrified expressions on everyone's faces as they realized that all the gigs were

suddenly gone. Knowing I was to blame was the worst sensation. 'Look, if it doesn't work out, fellas, we can get back together,' I added. But I have to try this.'
However, once the news had settled, the lads couldn't have been nicer or more giving about it. They knew no man could have turned it down. They were the best dudes ever. In fact, it's not an exaggeration to say that some of the happiest times of my life were spent with Geordie II.

Monday, 31 March, I should have been back at the Heaton Buffs social club, but instead I was in the E-Zee Hire practice facilities in King's Cross for a meeting with Peter and the band. He informed me that I'd be paid the same as the rest of the band and given 'per diems' anytime the band took me away from home. I had no idea what a per diem was, having never been paid one before - but Peter explained that it was cash-in-hand that I'd be given every day on the road to cover 'incidental expenditures'.

All I could think was, there has to be a catch. But there wasn't this time. I was suddenly in a different league.
Then Peter asked if there were any additional 'loose ends' that needed to be wrapped up.
When I told him about Red Bus, he made a mental note to find out what the terms of my contract were.

'Other than Red Bus, what else?' enquired Peter. 'Do you have a mortgage?'
'Yes, I do, on a house I don't even live in,' I replied.
'What is the balance?'
'I don't know. It cost £11,000, and I've been paying £70 a month as part of a court settlement.'
'Which bank is it with?'
'Well, it's a building society, not a bank, and it's Leeds Permanent.'
'OK, I'll phone them and pay it off.'
'What? 'Are you serious?'
'Of course. Is there anything else we should know?'

I was in shock at this point, but I remembered the prior night with the Geordie II men. I told Peter that I felt terrible for them since we'd had to cancel a month's worth of concerts, and they were all hard-working guys who could use the money. I told him I'd want to spend some of my pay to reimburse them for the month of April, which would at least cushion the blow while they looked for a replacement vocalist.

'Would £2,000 suffice?' Peter wondered.

I almost fell out of my chair. He wasn't kidding either; he subsequently brought me the cash in a brown envelope, and I took the men out to an Indian restaurant and distributed it over dinner. I couldn't have been happier to assist them after leaving the band so abruptly.

'Just one more thing,' Peter said. 'The boys want to make you a full member of AC/DC. I know you were simply an employee with Geordie, but this time we're seeking for entire dedication.'

'So... what does that mean?'

'It means you don't only get a wage. You get a fifth of the profits.'

'Are there any profits?' This was a strange language to me.

'Not yet, no,' Peter said.

'Oh,' I said. 'Well, never mind. Maybe if the new record goes well...'

'That looks reasonable.'

The news that I'd been hired as AC/DC's new singer arrived the next morning, April Fool's Day, by which time we were already practicing for the new album, which would be recorded at Polar Studios in Sweden.

Malcolm had offered me one of those yellow, wide-ruled legal pads after my business meeting with Peter and asked if I wanted to try my hand at writing lyrics for one of the riffs. Given how quickly things moved, my memory of when exactly this happened is vague - but most of the images taken of me at E-Zee Hire show me holding the pad, so I definitely put pen to paper for the first time there, even though most of the writing happened afterwards.

At first, Malcolm was only interested in a few sentences. But, at this point in my career, I'd only ever written two songs for Geordie.

Furthermore, considering the strength of the riff in question, I was going to have to come up with something truly unique.

The most difficult aspect of it all was trying to live up to Bon's songwriting heritage. From the nonstop double-entendres of 'Big Balls' to his happy and frankly hilarious depiction of a one-night affair with a nineteen-stone Tasmanian woman in 'Whole Lotta Rosie,' Bon had been the consummate working-class wordsmith. Of course, critics had missed the purpose of his songs when he was alive, but after his death, they suddenly discovered a newfound love for his marvelous way with words. Bon had never given a damn what people said. The establishment's sneers were presumably a badge of honor for him.

I had no idea if I could write anything even one-tenth as good as Bon's best songs. So, as soon as I was handed the legal pad and told to write anything down, I knew I wanted to locate a quiet place where I could use my brain. But, of course, I was in a rehearsal room in King's Cross, so my alternatives for peace and quiet were limited.

Brian, write about what you know. I told myself over and over. But, of course, cars were the only thing I was familiar with. Cars and ladies, to be specific. Actually... wait a minute, I was having an idea... 'She was a speedy machine,' I wrote, 'and she always maintained her motor clean.' 'She was the best damn woman I ever seen,' I added a moment later.
I was pleased with my performance. All I had to do now was compose two more verses and a chorus...

I was put up at the Holiday Inn, Swiss Cottage, throughout the week of the E-Zee Hire sessions, which felt very posh to me at the time. Phil was the only other member of the band who stayed there because everyone else had their own place.

Phil and I would return to the hotel after each long day of rehearsals and writing to get a quick bite to eat and a couple of beers. But I quickly found that, unlike me, Phil wasn't much of a talker, so after dinner we'd head back up to our rooms. It was unsettling. I began to worry if he knew something I didn't... like maybe the band was having second thoughts.

Phil must have spotted my worried expression as we entered the lift one night.
'Hey Jonna,' he continued, 'don't worry, mate, we love you.' 'You'll be alright, mate,' he added with a smile.
The relief was amazing because I had no idea on the inside. So, Phil, God bless you for expressing that. It meant everything to me.
The strangest aspect of joining AC/DC was suddenly becoming a part of a social circle where it was perfectly normal to hang out with other musicians - and not just any artists, but heroes of mine.
For example, on our second day at E-Zee Hire, in came Ozzy Osbourne, the guy I'd been listening to compulsively during my lunch breaks at Parsons. It was impossible for me to believe. And the strange thing was, he approached me, shook my hand, and wished me luck in my new position. Ozzy's words were all the more meaningful because he was a friend of Bon's. It was a life-changing experience for me, so thank you very much, Ozzy.

Meanwhile, the next night, Malcolm invited me to The Warrington, a bar in Maida Vale near a large roundabout, which was filled with musicians. So I went over there and had a pint with Malcolm and Cliff, and the next thing I knew, Mud's Les Gray was sitting at our table, saying, 'Hello Brian, congrats on the concert.'
It was excessive. It was an absolute whirlwind.

Another night, I went over to Malcolm's flat, and this fantastic bearded American guy came in, and Mal introduced him as 'Meet Brian, he's our new singer.' I rapidly became engrossed in talking with the man, who revealed that he'd survived a plane disaster in Mississippi. That's when I learned he was a member of Lynyrd Skynyrd. It was a tragic accident that killed half of the band. It has to be Gary Rossington. He was still struggling with his arm and walked with a limp.
There were numerous other instances like this. I wanted to jot down every detail so I wouldn't forget it - but I did.

Near the end of our time at E-Zee Hire, the band's favorite photographer, Robert Ellis, dropped by. Atlantic had asked him to do some publicity photos for the new album. It felt like months had passed, yet it was just April 4th, barely a week after I'd arrived in London and only three days after my hiring had been publicized.

Because Phil was nowhere to be found, we had to do several shots without him. Malcolm took Phil's place on the drum stool in one iconic shot. In another, I was sitting on the drum riser, wearing my '22' shirt and carrying a writing pad. When Phil arrived, we went outdoors to take some photographs against a brick wall.

When the photo shoot was finished, Peter came over to give some bad news: Polar Studios in Stockholm was no longer available since ABBA had just booked it.
'Where are we going?' Malcolm inquired.
'Compass Point,' shrugged Peter, to which everyone nodded and returned to work.
I waited a moment, too embarrassed to raise my hand in front of the lads, then took Peter away.
'Where is Compass Point?' I asked. I mean, at this point in my life, my knowledge of North East working men's clubs was unrivaled, but when it came to the world's most expensive and remote recording studios, I was ignorant.
'Well, I hate to be the bearer of bad news, Brian,' Peter remarked solemnly. 'But,' he grinned, 'we're going to drag you to The Bahamas.'

12. Greetings from Paradise

I hadn't even been at my new work for a week when I was whisked away to a tropical island in the West Indies. I could grow used to it, I reasoned.
Now, I should probably emphasize that Compass Point Studios was not quite as well-known in 1980 as it would become later. Chris Blackwell had created it barely three years before. He'd envisioned it as a haven where musicians like Island's own Bob Marley could work without the distractions of a big city.

Meanwhile, we'd been told that we'd have to share a portion of the studio with a New York band named Talking Heads.
Only two weeks before, I was performing on stage at Westerhope Club in front of a packed house of working men and women - and now I was travelling to the same recording studio as The Rolling Stones. It didn't feel real. And, in a way, it wasn't real because I still had to prove that Angus, Malcolm, and the others in the band made the correct decision in hiring me.

near least one thing hadn't changed: our seats were still near the back of the plane, just as they had been when Geordie traveled to Australia all those years before.
It was surreal being that close to the band for the first time. But Peter instantly broke the ice by pulling out a bag full of professional-grade Sony Walkmans - the ones that arrived in a special leather case - and handed them out. When I got mine, I felt like a kid on Christmas morning. At this point, the Walkman had only been on the market for roughly a year. It was the most technologically advanced item I'd ever seen - and when I put on the headphones and pressed play, the music quality was superior than almost anything I'd ever heard before. And, of course, the boys had brought along a cassette of the riff they'd been working on, so I spent the next six hours becoming acquainted with it and thinking of what I could sing over the top, all while downing as many beers as the flight attendants would allow.

I didn't expect to sleep a wink for the entire 4,000-mile flight, but the vodka kicked in, the lights went out, and my head dropped lifeless.

When we landed, it was still daylight. I stared out the window at the palm trees and the azure sea. It was paradise.
But it only took us five minutes after we stepped off the plane to run into problems.

The customs agents simply took one look at our long hair and denims and concluded that they didn't want us on their island, so they grabbed Malcolm and Angus aside and began questioning them about what was inside their guitar cases. It was the same power game played by soldiers all across the planet. But what the customs agents didn't realize was that Malcolm and Angus were fairly skilled at playing the same game - and they could out-intimidate just about anyone. As a result, a very long and tense stand-off developed, until the lead officer snapped and proclaimed that he was confiscating everything.

And with that, our instruments were confiscated, while Malcolm and Angus were brought away for further questioning. It took hours. Even though the lads were eventually released, their gear was not, including the guitars - including Malcolm's Gretsch and Angus' Gibson - that we needed to begin recording the album.
'Oh, don't worry about it, Brian,' Peter answered, 'that's just the way it goes.'

According to Peter, Malcolm and Angus disliked anyone wearing a uniform. When they were spoken to disrespectfully, their hackles rose. They'd put up this screen of quick and utter resistance at the first hint of difficulty, and if they thought they were being targeted, they wouldn't give an inch.

Customs authorities couldn't seize my suitcase since I didn't have one. I just had a carrying bag with two pairs of socks, three pairs of underpants, one pair of jeans, a denim jacket, three T-shirts (including the '22' one), and a cotton cap. That was it.

We were put up in a guesthouse just where the jungle ended and the beach began - and by beach, I don't mean Whitley Bay in Newcastle or Bondi Beach in Sydney. No, this was a true beach, a Robinson Crusoe beach, with powder-soft white sand, swaying palm palms, and the most exquisite turquoise blue water - despite the fact that our guesthouses were about as primitive as you could get.

Even though the studio was only about 150 yards away, our very large and strict Bahamian landlady advised us to use our Honda Civic rental car or jump on one of the studio's 50cc motorcycles to get there and back - and if we insisted on walking, she said to always go in a group and never at night. We assumed she was being overprotective on orders from Atlantic Records, who didn't want us walking off and becoming distracted. But we soon discovered that she had every reason to be concerned.

The Bahamas were experiencing a crime wave. Various types of boats were missing off the coast, stolen for drug trafficking. And there were these illegal bands hiding from the law in the forest. Buggers are dangerous.

Armed robberies, particularly house invasions, were also on the rise. Among the victims was Robert Palmer, who lived just across the street from the studio at the time. While he was in the studio one night, several thugs broke into his house, shot his dog, and held his poor mother and father at gunpoint, leaving everyone at Compass Point terrified.

Our landlady was not going to take any chances. She gave each of us a harpoon gun before even showing us to our rooms. She explained that they weren't for fishing, but in case any bad guys broke into our rooms while we were there. Then this guy walked in and handed each of us a machete as a backup in case the harpoon guns failed. Throughout my stay, I kept my harpoon gun by the entrance and my machete beneath my bed, fully anticipating to need both at some point.

My room... well, it wasn't exactly a room. It was more of a little cottage, about 12 feet by 12 feet, with a single bed, a handbasin, a small writing desk, and a toilet.
Obviously, there is no air conditioning or television.

Meanwhile, it was so hot and humid that I didn't know what to do. Of course, I hadn't brought any shorts, let alone swimming trunks, because the only shorts I owned were for football, and they were in Newcastle.
So, like everyone else in the band, I merely wore jeans.

Because of the confiscated equipment, we couldn't do anything for the first five days except put up Phil's drums. I ended up just wandering about the studio, looking for something to do, until I came across a pool table and a foosball table in the communal area. Then, just as I was getting into some games, the guys from Talking Heads showed up, taking a break from a session.

I thought, great, some fresh folks to talk to. The pub etiquette of putting a coin on the edge of the pool table perplexed David Byrne. I must have told him about it five times. But he kept staring at me as if I were speaking a different language, which, to be fair, I probably was.

Having said that, we did end up getting along well with Tina Weymouth and her husband Chris Frantz - Talking Heads' bassist and drummer. In fact, they later assisted us by filling in for Phil and Cliff when they went missing in the bush one day.

While we waited for our equipment, Malcolm awoke one morning to discover all of his money gone, so the police were called in, and an inquiry ensued, culminating with the landlady walking out on the beach with our tour manager Ian Jeffery, armed with harpoon guns. They never found the culprit, which was probably for the best because I didn't think they stood a chance against any of the local crooks.

Keith Emerson emerged and invited us out on his boat just as we were about to give up hope that our goods would never be found. Keith was fantastic. He had this amazing little speedboat with a tape player integrated into the dashboard, which I thought was the coolest thing imaginable. Cliff caught this big tuna on a later fishing trip, which was cause for great joy - until it was revealed that none of us had the foggiest notion how to prepare the bloody thing because the only tuna we'd ever seen before had come from cans.

Cliff ended up chopping the enormous monster into steaks about three or four inches thick, which he then chilled in the kitchen of the guesthouse. But there was a power outage that night, and when we went in the next morning, it looked like a murder scene. The fridge had effectively turned into an oven due to the heat and humidity, and the tuna had gone off - spectacularly - with blood gushing out all over the linoleum floor. It smelled like a fart that had passed its expiration date in there. So we left the landlady to fumigate the premises and moved to a more scented apartment, where we were relieved to hear that our equipment had finally cleared customs.

Finally, we could get on with what we'd come here to do.
And I was yanking on the leash to get started.
This is perhaps a good time to introduce Mutt Lange, who was engaged by the band to produce the album and collaborated on this occasion with sound engineer Tony Platt. I'd met both of them while working at E-Zee Hire in London, but they were only two of the numerous faces that had stopped by during the auditions.

Mutt wasn't exactly well-known at the time. He'd been in a couple bands around Johannesburg, so he understood his stuff, and it was the record business that discovered he was a bloody good producer. That's when he was brought in to produce Highway to Hell for AC/DC, and the boys liked what they heard.

Aside from his work ethic, Mutt had Malcolm's aptitude for near-superhuman hearing.
During one session, we were listening to a playback of one of the tracks when Malcolm asked, 'What's that noise?' Of fact, even after listening to it three or four times more, none of us could hear anything out of place. But then Mutt came in and picked up on the same noise. So he went through each track - bass, vocals, guitars, drums - reducing them down one by one, until there it was, a noise on one of the drum tracks that sounded like a little pair of castanets. But, of course, that prompted the question, what was causing it? To get to the bottom of it, we nearly flipped the studio upside down -

and lo and behold, it came out that a crab had walked in from the beach and was producing the undesired noise with its pincers in the corner of the room, which was picked up by the drum mics. I'm not sure how Malcolm or Mutt could have heard that over Angus' guitar.
My other early thoughts of Mutt were rather limited, owing to the fact that the morning after our gear arrived and we began working on the album, Malcolm came into my room with a request that made it difficult to concentrate on anything else.

'Hey Brian,' he continued, 'how did it go with those lyrics you were writing?'
'Oh, quite nice... I believe,' I said, recalling the words I'd composed about the 'quick machine' who 'kept her motor clean' - which was now virtually a complete song.
'That's great news,' Malcolm remarked. 'Can you keep on and finish the album?'
For a second, I assumed he was joking.
But he wasn't joking.

13. Back from Black

My plane touched down at Heathrow on May 5, a bank holiday Monday. That was the same day that the S.A.S. attacked the Iranian Embassy in London. REAGAN MADE A DEAL, AND THE IRANIANS RELEASED THE US HOSTAGES IN TEHRAN. It seemed strange to be abruptly back in the real world, with the BBC and ITV both broadcasting live coverage of this life-or-death raid.

Despite all of the labor, our lives in The Bahamas had been a relaxing breath of fresh air. We hadn't seen a single TV news broadcast or newspaper headline while we were working on the album. And then I was back in London, where everything and everyone had to get there quickly. Not that it bothered me. It was great to be back in the UK with the album finished, like being dropped into the home end of a football stadium just after your team scored a goal.

From the airport, I grabbed a taxi to Peter Mensch's office in Earl's Court. When he inquired how the recording went, I told him the truth: I had no idea. He stated he'd heard nice things but hadn't received official news - to which I replied, "Join the club."

That's when Peter opened his safe and pulled out the greatest wad of cash I'd ever seen in my life. It was my wage for the rest of the month, plus per diems for five weeks. It was utter lunacy. I mean, I'd just returned from five weeks in The Bahamas, having the time of my life - I felt like I should have given him money. I had nowhere to put all of the money. I was cramming it into my dirty laundry tote bag from the trip - and into every pocket of my pants and denim jacket that I could locate - like I'd just robbed a bank.

'What are you going to do now?' he inquired.
'Well, I guess I should go back to Newcastle and check on the business and the kids.'
'Nice one, Brian,' he said.
'How long before you require my services again?' I inquired.
'Perhaps a month?'

Then he inquired as to how I intended to return home. I told him I'd take a cab to King's Cross and then catch a train to see my brother - I couldn't wait to tell him all about The Bahamas. (And this time, I was able to pay my own first-class ticket.) Instead, he asked if I could do him a great favor. He'd just leased a Mercedes-Benz for the company, he continued, but the car they'd delivered him was a 'stick-shift' - meaning it had a manual transmission. And, as an American - or, more specifically, a New Yorker - Peter had only ever driven automatics, so he was terrified of driving the thing. Instead, it has been parked illegally outside since the day he bought it, with a growing collection of citations on its windscreen.

With that, he led me over to the window, where we gazed down on this absolutely fantastic Mercedes-Benz - but it was a somewhat dubious sewage yellow color - the kind of car that only captains of industry or football club directors could afford to drive.

'Would you mind looking after it for a while?' he asked as he handed me the keys. 'It has a full tank of gas, is properly insured, and has only a thousand miles on the clock.'

'Are you serious?'

'Look, I know it's a bother, but the parking penalties are costing me a lot.'

'Well . . .'

'Would you mind, please...? It would be a tremendous assistance...'

'All right. If you're insistent.'

I drove back up the A1 to Newcastle with the greatest shit-eating grin you've ever seen. The vehicle was spanking new. It still had the odor. Even the key fob was massive and hefty, made of the softest leather I'd ever felt and emblazoned with a three-pointed star. I drove as if I had stolen it.

All I could think was, I can't wait to take my children out in this and spoil them rotten. The hardest part of being away had been missing Joanne and Kala. And now I was driving home in a Mercedes, and I could afford to buy them whatever they desired.

My father was the first person to notice the automobile. He was unimpressed.

'That's a German automobile,' he hissed as I drove up outside No. 1 Beech Drive.
'No, Dad. It's, er... American.'
'It's bloody German.'
'Well, it was given to me by an American.'
At the very least, he allowed me drive him to his club in it. Of course, there were no assurances about what the future held - but in that moment, I felt like I'd 'made it'.
I went to the shop the next morning to see Ken.
'Oh, Brian, you're back,' he remarked.
'Is everything okay, Ken?' I enquired.
'Oh, absolutely. 'Despite the fact that it's been relatively quiet these last few weeks.' He pointed to the Mercedes. 'Do you want me to put a roof on that? 'Did one of the dealerships send it over?'
'That's my automobile, Ken,' I explained.
'What? Really?'
I smirked proudly.
'Would you like a roof on it?'
'Where is the Maxi?' I inquired, having noticed that it was vanished.
'Oh...' Ken dropped his face.
'Oh, what?'
'There was an accident.'
'What kind of accident?'
'It caught fire. With all of our materials in it. That's probably why it's been so silent...'

I shook my head and grumbled.
Several weeks passed in Newcastle. By that point, the Bahamas and the tropical storms had all faded into obscurity. I did receive one phone call from Olga from the Volga, but that was it.

It felt strangely natural at home, as if nothing had changed save the car sitting outside.
My mother and father had never heard of AC/DC and were scared that it would all be for naught. Maurice, on the other hand, was ecstatic.
But there was a valid explanation for the band's quiet.

What I didn't realize was that, aside from working on the mastering and artwork, Malcolm and Angus were dead serious about commencing 'Hells Bells' with a real tolling bell, then commissioning AC/DC's very own bell to accompany us on tour.
And it had all taken a lot of effort.

Tony Platt had scoured around for the exact bell he wanted to record, eventually deciding on the Denison Bell in the Carillon Tower at the Loughborough War Museum in Leicestershire. Then he'd leased a mobile recording device and gone over there to record it. But every time the bell rang, all the birds in the tower flew out, destroying the recording. And there was too much time between each ring of the bell to keep the birds away. Finally, Tony had to give up and wait for the band's own bell to be produced.

The John Taylor & Co Foundry, also in Loughborough, had been chosen to cast the bell. It weighed 2,000 pounds, or exactly one ton, and had the AC/DC emblem and song title stamped on the side. The bell was built just in time to meet Atlantic Records' deadline, but there was a problem: it was smaller than the Denison Bell, thus the tone wasn't quite perfect. Tony, being a technological genius, soon found a solution - he simply slowed the tape down to half speed, making it a perfect match. Tony also asked the craftsman who had cast the 'Hell's Bell' to ring it for the final recording, which is still played all over the world today.

I later learned that while the Hell's Bell was still in the foundry, workers suspended it from the ceiling and tapped it with a forklift truck to signal when it was time for a tea break.
So, for a period, AC/DC had essentially commissioned the world's most expensive dinner gong.
Finally... a box arrived for me.

It was one of the very first pressings of Back in Black. After removing the LP from its protective cardboard sleeve, I just stared at it for what felt like hours. The cover was all black, with the AC/DC logo in grey outline and the title in faded capital letters underneath. It was so basic... and yet so incredible.

I was desperate to hear how it sounded, but I had nothing to play it on because my parents still only had their Rediffusion radio. So I called Derek Rootham, Geordie's guitarist, who had a decent setup at home.

'Oh, you're back, aren't you?' he inquired. 'So, what have you been up to all this time?'
'Well, if I can use your record player,' I explained, 'you can hear for yourself...'
I was in Derek's living room a few hours later, listening to Back in Black on the turntable. The first tune, of course, was 'Hells Bells,' which starts with a bell, then Malcolm's main riff, then slowly builds with Phil's bass drum and cymbals until it eventually gets going, with my vocals coming in about the minute-and-a-half mark. That's a long time, and for a brief minute, I believed they'd forgotten about me. All the while, I'm thinking to myself, this sounds fucking amazing. I mean, I was getting chills. But then I noticed Derek frowning and shaking his head, and when we got to the 'Won't take no prisoners' line, he let out a tiny scream and remarked, 'Ooh Jonna, that's way too high. 'Man, you're singing far too high!'
'What?'
'Way up there. I'll take you out for a pint.'

We went for a pint after that little kick in the belly!
We started preparing for the Back in Black Tour at the New Victoria Theatre, opposite Victoria Station in London, in late June, about two months after I returned from The Bahamas. (It is now the Apollo Victoria.) We just had four days to get our sh*t together. Following that, a 'warm-up tour' in only two countries - Belgium and the Netherlands - was planned, with the main North American tour to coincide with the album's release due to begin on July 13 in Edmonton, Canada.

The rehearsals' major goal was to break in the material while simultaneously breaking in... me. After all, the band had been playing the old tunes for years and everyone recognized them. But, with the exception of 'Whole Lotta Rosie' and 'Highway to Hell,' all were unfamiliar to me. It was a lot to ask. We'd upload one or two new songs every couple weeks to Geordie II. But now I had to memorize songs from the band's previous six albums, as well as the majority of the new material on Back in Black, which I'd only ever sung in the studio before.

Meanwhile, the crew began assembling our set as rehearsals progressed, until a delivery crew arrived with the Hell's Bell - and what a magnificent beast it was. When this monster talked, it was both scary and magical, as well as harsh and sensual. It looked incredible when it was hauled into position in the midst of the lighting rig. But we wouldn't see it again for quite some time. When the rehearsals were finished, the bell was shipped to Canada to begin the North American tour, while we stayed in Europe for the warm-up shows.

On June 29, 1980, the first gig of the warm-up tour - and my first show as AC/DC's new lead singer - took place in Namur, about an hour south-east of Brussels. The location was one of the Palais des Expositions' halls. Because the performance had not been highly advertised, we were expecting only approximately 2,000 attendees. And by not widely advertised, I mean they'd kept it a secret so we could get our bearings before playing in front of a genuine arena-sized crowd.

I tried to remain calm and take everything in, but I couldn't eat. I couldn't stay seated. My heart was racing. I had to pee all the time.
We were due to perform at 8.30 p.m., but Peter came in with Ian Jeffery, the tour manager, and said, 'Hold on' - a thousand more people than expected had arrived, so they needed to install extra seats in the hall. This was simple to accomplish in a convention center because the walls could be shifted.

Take it easy, Brian; you've got plenty of time.
The rest of the lads didn't appear to mind. They just sat there chatting, drinking beer and saying, 'Okay, Brian?' and me saying, 'yes, yes, OK,' as my mind was overloaded with new music, new words, and anxiety of messing up.

I really wanted to get out there and charge over the top with the lads. I'd assumed this was going to be a tiny, low-key show in case something went wrong. No, they were allowing an extra thousand people in, so we had to wait. After about a half-hour, Peter and Ian returned to inform that several thousand more individuals had arrived. Fuck. There had to be some form of word-of-mouth going on. And, of course, Peter desired to move the walls once more. So he did... just in time for the next influx of fans. Anyway, this went on for what felt like an entire school arithmetic class on a beautiful day, until it was eventually - by now very late - time for the concert.

We were going to be playing in front of a nearly full house.
Angus was the first to run out, and the crowd let out an audible, guttural yell that sent shivers down my spine. It was very deafening and appeared to last forever. And it was at that moment that I felt the full weight of the work I'd taken on for the first time. Then I remembered being in the plane's door for my first leap, and how I felt standing there, and there I was again. Only this time I wasn't in any danger...

Everything went silent in my head. Just like my first plunge from that plane, I could see the lights. I felt prepared. That's my signal. This time I had to force myself out. I've never felt such a rush. Ever. And the audience, the music, and the band served as my parachute.

14. The Final Section before the End

There's not much else to say about Back in Black that hasn't already been said. All I can tell is that when I came out on stage in Namur that night, the audience's support was incredible. I could see banners and signs with words like 'R.I.P. Bon' and 'Good luck, Brian' everywhere I looked. A part of me felt that the fans would never accept another vocalist in Bon's place. But there I was, being welcomed. I'll be eternally thankful to AC/DC fans for that - for giving me a chance.

Thank you, thank you, thank you...
When I think back, it's hard to believe - in fact, I had to double-check it - but that first gig featured no fewer than seven songs from Back in Black, an album that wouldn't be out for another four or five weeks. We did four of those songs in a row after the midway point of 'Highway to Hell' - 'What Do You Do for Money Honey,' 'Rock and Roll Ain't Noise Pollution,' 'Shoot to Thrill,' and 'Givin' the Dog a Bone'.

As previously said, AC/DC has always been an all-or-nothing band.
What's really astonishing is that the audience stayed seated and listened, completely absorbing every note - and by the second chorus of 'Have a Drink on Me,' they were singing it back to us. We all believed in the record, of course, but this was beyond anything we could have imagined. By the time we got to 'Whole Lotta Rosie,' the chants of 'Angus' between the opening riffs were so loud that the entire structure began to tremble. Then we finished with 'Rocker' - coming back for an encore of 'Shake a Leg', then 'Let There Be Rock'. It was the first and final time we performed 'Shake a Leg' live.

I did, however, make a major blunder that night.
We were due to play a couple of oldies, 'Shot Down in Flames' and 'Hell Ain't a Bad Place to Be', after the opener of 'Hells Bells', which was now on a cargo ship to Canada. But I was so scared that I started with 'Hell Ain't a Bad Place to Be'... while the band was playing 'Shot Down in Flames'. Thankfully, the music was so loud that no one could hear me - except for the fans in the first few rows, who

were staring at me, like, what the fuck are you doing? But no one else seemed to mind. And by the time 'Hell Ain't a Bad Place to Be' started for real, I'd already done one run-through - albeit to the wrong music - so I just sang it again. And then everything was fine.

Meanwhile, in the dressing room after the show, none of us could find any words - literally. We were all gasping for air, sweat running down our faces. You can't even drink a beer in that situation; you'd just spew it up.

Cliff, who was always the coolest person in the room, was smoking a tab and staring at me. 'Are you all okay, Jonna?'
'Brilliant, mate,' I exclaimed.
Outside, we could still hear the throng yelling and clapping for more.
There was no need for any further discussion.
The fans stated everything that needed to be said.
What a night.
The most fulfilling aspect of Back in Black's success was that it allowed me to give back to the people who had always been there for me, most notably my children, my mother and father, my brother Maurice, sister Julie, and brother Victor.

When the royalty checks started pouring in, I bought my parents their own house - halfway up Whickham Bank, adjacent to Dunston, with magnificent views of Newcastle. My father was worried about the concept, believing that if he didn't pay his council rent, the guys at his club would stop talking to him. But he eventually changed his mind... and, of course, his friends were delighted for him in the end.
A few years later, I was also able to assist Maurice in obtaining employment as a chef. He'd been going through a hard patch after his marriage collapsed, so I asked the boys if they'd consider giving him a month's trial. And, of course, the moment he began, everyone fell in love with him, as they usually do. He even went on to win the band's'most valuable roadie' accolade. It was the least I could do for Maurice. In fact, I still owe him a new cap from that gig at Lobley Hill.

I won't lie: Australia was the most difficult leg of the Back in Black Tour for me. Bon wasn't simply famous in Australia. He'd been an icon, a national treasure. They'd grown up with him. The Valentines is the first episode. Then in Fraternity.

Our first performance was in Perth's Entertainment Centre, one of the country's largest arenas. This was very much Bon territory, with his hometown of Fremantle only a few miles away. To say the least, I was nervous. But no sooner had we landed than Peter was delivered a message from a member of the crew that said, 'Mrs. Scott would really like to meet Brian.' I felt a feeling of relief as soon as I heard it, because I knew that seeing AC/DC in town would remind Bon's mother of her loss, which must have been devastating. It had been almost a year since Bon's death.

I ended up spending the afternoon drinking numerous cups of tea with Mrs. Scott - or Isa - and Bon's brothers, Derek and Graeme. She was the most wonderful woman, still with her thick Scottish accent. I later learnt that Malcolm was the one who called her first with the news of Bon's murder because he was afraid the British media would get to her first. That was so Malcolm. Such a gentleman. I mean, the courage it must have taken to make that decision...

The finest part of my time with Isa was hearing her stories about Bon when he was younger. 'Aye, Ronald was a wee terror, he wouldn't wear shoes, he was constantly gettin' intae trouble, he was fearless,' she explained.

Of course, I thanked her, but it didn't seem enough.
Derek and Graeme also dropped the bombshell that Bon was the guy in Fang who I'd met on that frigid night in Torquay. That was something I couldn't quite wrap my brain around. I still can't... But I'm glad I met Bon at least once, and that it meant enough to him to tell his family about it when he came home.

Anyway, after we'd spoken and laughed some more, I had to go to the show, and Isa joined me. We dedicated 'High Voltage' to her, and the guys in the band felt 'it' that night. I'm not sure what 'it' was, but it felt good.

I'll conclude with a scene that encapsulates everything about the insane year in which Back in Black was released.

We were performing at Long Beach Arena, just outside of Los Angeles, on September 4th. With a capacity of just under 15,000 people, it was definitely one of the largest venues I'd ever played in. There was a limo traffic congestion outside, a helicopter hovering overhead with AC/DC lit up beneath it, and, of course, the RMS Queen Mary anchored right there on the shore, all lit up. Just the most thrilling setting for a rock'n'roll event - and one of the first indications that the album was growing into something much, much bigger than any of us could have dreamed.

We were each given our own limo to transport us to the concert that night - just for the show - and when I went into mine, I greeted hello to the driver and inquired how he was doing.

'Aye, no' bad, thank you very much.'

'You're a long way from home, aren't you?' I told him, surprised.

'Aye, well,' he explained, 'I came over with a band, and we're still trying to get a deal, make things happen.'

'Well, I wish you the best of luck, pal,' I said.

After a little pause, he stated, 'Actually, I'm a vocalist like yerself...'

'Really?' I said. 'What is the name of your band?'

'Marmalade,' he said.

'What?!!' I couldn't believe it. Not only was I familiar with Marmalade, but I also knew who their singer was. Alan Whitehead was his given name. Marmalade weren't simply some unsigned band with a bunch of demo tapes. They'd been a major act, reaching No. 1 in the UK charts. They'd been everywhere for a while. But, of course, that was - what? - eleven years ago.

'Alan?!' I exclaimed.

'Yeah!'

'Fuck me!'

'I'm just doing this to pay the rent,' Alan explained. 'At the very least, I still get to hang around with musicians.'

'Well, you might not believe this, but a few months ago, I was living with my parents and fitting vinyl car roofs for a living,' I explained. So everything is possible...'

We had a nice chuckle over it, then chatted nonstop all the way to the arena.

Never give up.

Printed in Great Britain
by Amazon